FORTY
LESSONS AND EXE
IN
GRAMMAR AND LANGUAGE

FORTY
LESSONS AND EXERCISES
IN
GRAMMAR AND LANGUAGE

R. E. HOUSEMAN, M.A., M.ED.
and
J. D. BENTLEY, M.A.

HULTON EDUCATIONAL PUBLICATIONS

ISBN 0 7175 0190 6 – Pupil's book
0 7175 0191 4 – With Answers

First published 1960 by
HULTON EDUCATIONAL PUBLICATIONS LTD.
Raans Road, Amersham, Bucks.
Reproduced, printed and bound in Great Britain by
Richard Clay (Bungay) Ltd.

INTRODUCTION

For a number of years now the study of syntax and language structure has been out of fashion in some schools, where it is thought that effective communication can be taught more by precept and experience. However, many teachers are finding that their pupils are handicapped in their powers of expression and comprehension unless they have some basic understanding of how language works and how it is put together. This revised edition of a popular text-book aims to meet those needs.

The TEACHER'S ANSWER BOOK makes possible speedy and accurate marking.

CONTENTS

Lesson   *Page*

1. WORDS: VOCABULARY   9
2. SENTENCES AND PHRASES   12
3. PARTS OF SPEECH   15
4. NOUNS: COMMON, PROPER, COLLECTIVE, ABSTRACT   20
5. NOUNS: NUMBER AND GENDER   23
6. PRONOUNS: PERSONAL, RELATIVE, POSSESSIVE   25
7. PRONOUNS: INTERROGATIVE, DEMONSTRATIVE, INDEFINITE   29
8. ADJECTIVES: DEMONSTRATIVE, POSSESSIVE, QUALITY, QUANTITY, INTERROGATIVE   33
9. THE ARTICLES: COMPARISON OF ADJECTIVES   36
10. VERBS: TRANSITIVE AND INTRANSITIVE, ACTIVE AND PASSIVE, AUXILIARY VERBS   39
11. VERBS: MOOD, TENSE, NUMBER, PERSON, INFINITIVE, PARTICIPLES   43
12. REVISION TEST (1)   47
13. SPECIAL FORMS OF VERBS   50
14. ADVERBS: CLASSES   56
15. ADVERBIAL PHRASES   59
16. PREPOSITIONS (1)   62
17. PREPOSITIONS (2)   66
18. CONJUNCTIONS AND INTERJECTIONS   69
19. COMMON MISTAKES (1) NOUNS, PRONOUNS   72
20. COMMON MISTAKES (2) ADJECTIVES, ADVERBS   76
21. REVISION TEST (2)   80
22. PUNCTUATION   84
23. DIRECT AND INDIRECT OR REPORTED SPEECH   88

Lesson	*Page*
24. PREFIXES AND SUFFIXES	92
25. SOME SPELLING RULES	96
26. SOME WORDS OFTEN CONFUSED	101
27. THE PHRASE AND CLAUSE	109
28. COMMON EXPRESSIONS	113
29. SOME DEVICES USED IN WRITING	116
30. SYNONYMS, ANTONYMS, HOMONYMS	120
31. REVISION TEST (3)	125
32. SIMPLE ANALYSIS AND PARSING	129
33. MORE COMMON MISTAKES (1)	132
34. MORE COMMON MISTAKES (2)	135
35. ROOTS: MORE SUFFIXES AND PREFIXES	139
36. THE USE OF THE DICTIONARY	144
37. IDIOMS, COLLOQUIALISMS, CLICHÉS AND SLANG	147
38. PROVERBS	151
39. WHAT WE HAVE LEARNT	156
40. GENERAL REVISION TEST	163

WORDS

Vocabulary

WORDS are bricks with which we build language. It is most important to choose a suitable word for the occasion. A word once spoken can never be recalled. Here are points to bear in mind:

We should use a *simple* rather than a long word. We should call a spade a "spade" and not "a well-known agricultural implement".

A word ought to be *precise*. No two words in the English language mean exactly the same thing, but many words have slightly different shades of meaning, e.g.: abandon, leave, forsake, desert, relinquish, give up.

Vagueness is a common fault. We often say "It was a nice day" when we may mean "It was a fine warm day" or "It was an enjoyable jolly day" or "It was a quiet peaceful day".

Avoid *repetition*. Do not use the same word over and over again. Use a word of similar meaning.

Do not misuse words, as in: "He *learns* me arithmetic". This should be: "He *teaches* me arithmetic", as it is the teacher who teaches and the pupil who ought to *learn*.

Avoid the use of slang expressions (such as *super*, *great*, *smashing*, *fabulous*, *fantastic*) on unsuitable occasions. See page 150.

EXERCISES

1. Write out the following sentences using a more suitable word than *nice*:

(a) We have been having *nice* weather lately.
(b) We had a *nice* dinner today.
(c) She was very *nice* to me.
(d) What a *nice* dress you are wearing!
(e) How *nice* it is to see you again!

Another overworked word is *said*. Many people use this word far too often in their writing. This does not mean we must *never* use this word, but it tells us nothing about the mood of the speaker and often better words can be used instead

2. In these sentences substitute another suitable word for *said*:

(a) In answer to my question, he *said* that he could not come.
(b) He *said* "Good gracious! I have lost my satchel".
(c) He *said* in a low voice, "They are over there".
(d) She *said* that I should go at once.
(e) My mother *said* over and over again that I must not be late.
(f) He *said* that he could play football better than anyone else.

VOCABULARY is simply a person's stock of words. People's vocabularies naturally vary as much as their character or appearance. Vocabulary depends largely upon one's education, occupation and surroundings. One famous author is said to have a working vocabulary of 30,000 words. A waitress manages on about 7,000 words, and people in trades or professions tend to use words which relate to their own special work. The smallest number of words we need to use has been estimated at about 850, but few of us would be content with this.

How to Increase Our Vocabulary:

By listening to others, to speakers on radio and television, to teachers, parents and friends.

By reading, understanding and constantly using a dictionary.

To add to our stock of words, we can prepare lists of pairs of *opposite* meaning, such as, "guilty" and "innocent", "visible" and "invisible", or words of *similar* meaning, such as "hate", "despise", "dislike", or "love", "like", "adore", etc.

In writing composition, it is a good plan to jot down all the words we can think of associated with the subject. If we then arrange and sort them out afterwards, we shall have plenty of ideas upon which to base the composition.

3. Write down as many words as possible associated with:

(a) A railway station.   (d) Road safety.
(b) A scene at the seaside.   (e) A supermarket.
(c) A post office.   (f) An airport.

4. Write down as many words as you can think of which would most likely form part of the everyday vocabulary of any of the following:

(a) A farmer.   (e) A teacher.
(b) A postman.   (f) A milkman.
(c) A cook.   (g) A grocer.
(d) A bus driver.   (h) A nurse.

We can form new words by adding a single letter or syllable (called a *prefix*) to the beginning of a word, or we can put it at the end of a word (called a *suffix*), e.g.:

WORD	*SYLLABLE IN FRONT* *(Prefix)*	*NEW WORD*
turn	re	return
WORD	*WORD OR SYLLABLE* *AT END (Suffix)*	*NEW WORD*
child	hood	childhood

5. Here are some prefixes:
bi-, mis-, im-, en-, dis-,
   Here are some words:
port, trust, cycle, agree, fold.
   Add the right prefixes to the words to form new words.

6. Here are some suffixes:
-our, -ier, -ize, -ence, -eer.
   In the same way, add the right suffix to the following words to make new words:
exist, cash, equal, clam, auction.

7. Here are some prefixes and suffixes mixed up:
ab (pref.), er (suff.), bene (pref.), ice (suff.), over (pref.), ling (suff.).

Attach these in front or at the end of the following words to make a new word:
fit, coat, just, normal, contain, duck.

LESSON 2

SENTENCES AND PHRASES

A SENTENCE is a complete thought expressed in words. A simple sentence must be complete in itself. It should contain a SUBJECT or name, and a PREDICATE, or what is said about the subject. It generally begins with a capital letter and must end with a full stop, question mark or exclamation mark. A PHRASE is a group of words making sense, *but not complete sense.*

There are several kinds of sentence:

1. Statements: "Tom wrote the letter."
   "Down came the rain."
2. Questions: "Why are you here?"
3. Commands: "Go away."
4. Requests: "Please close the door."
   "Will you kindly phone me?"
5. Desires or Wishes: "I wish 1 knew his name."
6. Exclamations: "What a fright he gave us!"

The person or thing that does the action of a verb is called the SUBJECT of the verb.

e.g.: *Tom* wrote the letter.

Some verbs are not verbs of action:

e.g.: I have a cold.
      She heard a noise.
      This book is mine.
      Our dog died yesterday.

The person or thing that becomes, dies, has, hears, is, etc., is the SUBJECT of the verb. In those sentences the SUBJECTS are "I", "She", "This book", "Our dog".

In sentences such as "The letter was written by Tom", although the person who did the action of the verb—who wrote the letter—was Tom, we look specially at the verb "was" and we consider "The letter" as the SUBJECT of "was written".

Similarly in these sentences, "We were surprised by his sudden appearance" and "Their house will be built by the firm of Perkins & Sons", the SUBJECTS are "We" and "Their house".

In most sentences the subject comes before the verb, but in some sentences it may come after.

e.g.: "Why are you here?"
Down came the rain.

In some sentences the subject may not actually be expressed, but it is understood.

e.g.: "Go away."—"(You) go away."

The other words in the sentence—the words which tell us what the subject does or has or is—are called the PREDICATE of the sentence.

SUBJECT	PREDICATE
Tom	wrote the letter.
I	have a cold.
Our dog	died yesterday.
The rain	came down.

EXERCISES

1. State only the subject in these sentences:
(a) Here comes the bus.
(b) Long live the Queen.
(c) When was that bridge built?
(d) Will you please lend me your book?
(e) What a splendid house they have bought!

13

2. State which kind of sentence each is:

(a) Here comes the bus.
(b) When was that bridge built?
(c) Will you please lend me your book?
(d) He was watching the television programme.
(e) Come here at once.
(f) I wish I were (*or* was) going to the cinema with you.
(g) What a splendid house they have bought!

3. State the subjects and also the predicates in these sentences:

(a) Here comes the bus.
(b) These apples are not for sale.
(c) The shop will open at 8 a.m.
(d) He was watching the television programme.
(e) Down came the rain.
(f) Have you change for this pound note?
(g) Come here at once.

4. Write down these SUBJECTS, and against each subject write the most suitable of these PREDICATES:

SUBJECTS	PREDICATES
(a) Our dog	has three sides.
(b) Lions	help to keep law and order.
(c) A sparrow	exceeded the speed limit.
(d) The old soldier	disappeared into a tiny hole in the floor.
(e) The motorists	are wild animals.
(f) The policemen	hopped along the windowsill for the breadcrumbs.
(g) The mouse	barks at the moon.
(h) A triangle	has a wooden leg.

5. Answer these questions with statements:

(a) What is the capital of France?
(b) What is your favourite lesson?
(c) Where do you live?
(d) What would you like to be when you grow up?

6. Suggest questions which could receive these answers:

(a) I am twelve years old.
(b) I am very well, thank you.
(c) I have two sisters and one brother.
(d) We had fine weather for the whole month.

A PHRASE is a sensible group of words without SUBJECT or PREDICATE, e.g.: "in the rain", "twelve new cars", "having lost all the money".

Some groups of words are not phrases because they make no sense, e.g.: "rabbit birthday under", "being she ill".

Phrases can be made into sentences by the addition of other words: "He stood *in the rain.*"

7. State which of the following are SENTENCES and which are PHRASES:

(a) Chuckling with glee.
(b) She saw Esau.
(c) Very close to the wall.
(d) A bright light.
(e) Speak clearly.
(f) Birds fly.
(g) Over she went.
(h) With a nod of the head.
(i) Milk is a food.
(j) Rubbing his hands.
(k) It is a rainy day.
(l) Under a spreading chestnut tree.

LESSON 3

PARTS OF SPEECH

In English we usually classify words into PARTS OF SPEECH, but we should remember that it is the FUNCTION (OR JOB) of a word in a sentence that determines what part of speech the word is.

The eight classes are:

NOUNS, PRONOUNS, VERBS, ADJECTIVES, ADVERBS, PREPOSITIONS and CONJUNCTIONS.

(*Note:* Some people do not regard the INTERJECTION—a word meaning "thrown into" a sentence, e.g.: "Oh!", "Well!", "Ugh!"—as a part of speech, but it is usual to include it.)

A word, however, may be almost any part of speech. The same word may be a verb, noun, adverb, or adjective. e.g.:

(a) He will *fast* during Lent.
(b) After several days he broke his *fast*.
(c) He works *fast*.
(d) Catherine is a *fast* worker.

> In (a) the word *fast* is a verb.
> In (b) it is a noun.
> In (c) it is an adverb.
> In (d) it is an adjective.

So you see we must decide what part of speech a word is by the work it does in the sentence.

Here are the eight classes into which we divide words:
1. NOUNS are words that name **persons, places, things or ideas.**

2. PRONOUNS are words **used instead of nouns,** e.g.: *I, they, she, he, it.*
   Pronouns have two main uses.

(a) We avoid repeating a noun, e.g.: When my brother met his wife, *he* told *her* the news and *they* came to Manchester.
(b) We can mention persons or things without actually naming them, e.g.:
   That is his.
   Nobody knows much about *them.*
   Everyone was present.

3. ADJECTIVES **qualify nouns or pronouns,** e.g.: A *sour* apple. An *interesting* story. Give me *that* pen. The ladder is *unsafe.*

4. VERBS are **doing, saying,** or **telling** words, e.g.: I *came*, I *saw*, I *conquered.*

16

Every sentence must contain a verb. Most verbs denote an action, e.g.: He *ran* home. The sun *sets* at 6 p.m. The milkman *brings* milk.

Some verbs denote a state or circumstance, e.g.: He *seems* happy. The boy *became* a plumber.

5. ADVERBS **qualify or restrict the meaning of verbs, adjectives** or *other adverbs.* They may sometimes qualify even prepositions and conjunctions, but *never* nouns or pronouns.

(a) Adverbs used with verbs. He came *quickly*. He walked *fast*.
(b) Adverbs used with adjectives. She was *extremely* puzzled. She was a *very* lazy girl.
(c) Adverbs used with other adverbs. She behaved *quite* well. Why did he go *so* slowly?

Adverbs give answers to the questions: *How? When? Where? Why? To what degree?*

Many adverbs are formed from adjectives by adding the suffix "-ly", e.g.: slow, *slowly*; bright, *brightly*.

6. PREPOSITIONS **show the relation of nouns and pronouns to other words,** e.g. *in, through, of, about, across.*

Prepositions must be followed by a noun or pronoun which they are said to govern:

She was the tallest girl *in* the family.
Share these *among* yourselves.
The garage is *behind* the house.

7. CONJUNCTIONS join together words or groups of words. The most common are *and, but, so, if, whether, that, either, or neither, nor.* Some of those words can be used as other parts of speech, but when they join words or sentences they are conjunctions.

8. INTERJECTIONS and PARTICLES are exclamations; or cries of emotion; or words expressing agreement, obedience, disagreement, refusal. Some are "Oh!", "Indeed!", "Alas!", "Yes", "No".

EXERCISES

1. State the part of speech of each word in italics in these sentences:

(a) He ran *swiftly* along the street.

(b) I saw a *high* tower.

(c) London is the largest *city* in Britain.

(d) Brian was late because *he* overslept.

(e) It was a cold *and* rainy night.

(f) I could not see *through* the hedge.

(g) The wind *blew* fiercely.

(h) *Ah!* That was a mistake.

(i) *Philip* has become an excellent footballer.

(j) I told him *that* I would meet him at noon.

(k) They live *here.*

(l) The road is *slippery* after the rain.

2. The same word can be almost any part of speech. State the part of speech of each word in italics:

(a) I can *pitch* the ball across the field.

(b) Can you *pitch* a tent?

(c) The length of a cricket *pitch* is twenty-two yards.

(d) It was *pitch* dark.

(e) The night was as black as *pitch.*

(f) It's a *long* lane that has no turning.

(g) I *long* for your return.

(h) Will you be *long?*

3. Write out the PRONOUNS in the following sentences:

(a) He hurt his leg yesterday.

(b) They went for a walk and the dog followed behind them.

(c) Did you meet your friend before we met ours?

(d) The Queen herself was present, but she did not stay long.

(e) It was my satchel that was found on the bus which left school at 4.15 p.m.

18

4. Here is a list of ADJECTIVES:

delicious, soft, five, small, tall, sharp.

   Insert the most suitable adjective in these sentences:

(a) The Eiffel Tower is a —— building.
(b) There were —— boys playing in the yard.
(c) It was —— ice cream.
(d) He made a —— hole in the wall.
(e) It was a —— knife.
(f) A cat has —— fur.

5. Use each of the VERBS given in the list below, once only, to complete the sentences:

sang, flew, ploughed, dug, laughed, looked, saved, smiled.

(a) He —— me from drowning.
(b) He —— the garden.
(c) She —— broadly.
(d) He —— tunefully.
(e) He —— heartily.
(f) The bird —— quickly.
(g) He —— the field.
(h) He —— over his shoulder.

6. Pick out the ADVERBS in these sentences and say which verb each adverb qualifies:

(a) She danced gracefully.
(b) He went abroad.
(c) I shall always remember this.
(d) They nearly succeeded.

7. Pick out the PREPOSITIONS and CONJUNCTIONS in these sentences:

(a) Put it on the table when you have finished.
(b) He fell and hurt his knee on a stone.
(c) They tried hard, but could not push the car out of the mud.
(d) The cake was shared between Joan and Peter.
(e) He wanted neither eggs nor bacon for his breakfast.

19

NOUNS

Common, Proper, Collective, Abstract

NOUNS are naming words. The word NOUN comes from the Latin *nomen* (= a name).

There are two main classes of nouns: COMMON and PROPER.

A COMMON NOUN is the name an object has in common with other objects of the same class. The word "common" really means "shared by all". *Ship, bicycle, animal, pen, postman, lake* are some common nouns.

PROPER NOUNS are the names of special people, places, nationalities, languages, or things. The word PROPER comes from the Latin *proprius* (= own); so, if you are in doubt, ask yourself whether the noun has its own special name and qualities which distinguish it from other nouns of the same class; if it has, it is a PROPER NOUN.

A PROPER NOUN should begin with a capital letter. Thus, the names of months and days should be written with capital letters. Your forename or Christian name, such as John or Mary, as well as your surname, Smith or White or Robinson, must begin with capital letters, and so must the name of your town, village, street, and house.

Abbreviations of PROPER NOUNS are usually written in capital letters, such as A.A. (Automobile Association), Dr. (Doctor); but abbreviations of COMMON NOUNS usually begin with small letters, e.g.: vb. (verb), yrs. (years).

There are three types of COMMON NOUN, namely, ORDINARY CLASS NOUNS, COLLECTIVE NOUNS, ABSTRACT NOUNS.

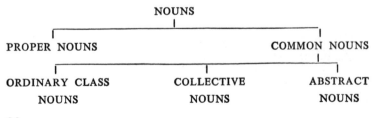

```
                        NOUNS
                          |
  ┌───────────────────────────────────────────────┐
PROPER NOUNS                              COMMON NOUNS
                                                |
      ┌──────────────────────┬─────────────────────┐
ORDINARY CLASS          COLLECTIVE            ABSTRACT
   NOUNS                  NOUNS                 NOUNS
```

COLLECTIVE NOUNS are used for collections or groups of people, things, or animals, e.g.: *crowd, flock, committee, class, suit.*

ABSTRACT NOUNS are the names of qualities, conditions, emotions, actions, e.g.: *goodness, poverty, anger, speed, patience, boyhood, strength.*

EXERCISES

1. Pick out all the COMMON NOUNS in this:
"Then a mile of warm sea-scented beach;
   Three fields to cross till a farm appears;
   A tap at the pane, the quick sharp scratch
   And blue spurt of a lighted match,
   And a voice less loud, through its joys and fears,
   Than the two hearts beating each to each."

2. Pick out the PROPER NOUNS in these sentences and write them down, beginning with capital letters:
(a) john lives in manchester.
(b) I saw a new rolls-royce last tuesday.
(c) march is usually a windy month.
(d) I was reading the bible.
(e) marjorie robertson is learning french.
(f) brussels is the capital of belgium.

3. (a) Write down as many forenames or Christian names of boys as you can, beginning with the letter A. These will all be PROPER NOUNS.
(b) Write down as many girls' names as you can, beginning with the letter M. These will all be PROPER NOUNS.

4. Choose the right noun from these COLLECTIVE NOUNS to use in these sentences:
cast, crew, flight, flock, herd, mob, pack, squad, suite, swarm:
(a) The whole —— of cards fell to the floor.

(b) The pilot and co-pilot and other members of the —— of the aircraft walked across to the hangar.

(c) I saw a large —— of seagulls.

(d) Two important members of the —— were ill, so the other actors could not proceed with the play.

(e) A —— of flies came in through the window.

(f) What a fine —— of cattle the farmer has!

(g) Mrs. Taylor has bought a lovely new —— of furniture for her dining-room.

(h) The —— of rioters tried to smash down the door of the embassy, but a —— of police managed to keep them away.

(i) The child slipped at the top of the stairs and tumbled down the whole —— of stairs.

5. In this passage the wrong COLLECTIVE NOUNS are used with the groups of people or things. Sort out the COLLECTIVE NOUNS and put them in their right places:

"The whole *forest* of doctors and nurses at the hospital had to give their qualifications and experience on a form. One doctor, who objected to this form, wrote a *staff* of lies on it—that he had once accompanied a *congregation* of musicians abroad—he had once preached a sermon to a large *pack* in church on Sunday— he had worked as a woodman cutting down trees in a Canadian *orchestra*."

6. Give the ABSTRACT NOUNS related to the ordinary class nouns of people, e.g.: *boy—boyhood, farmer—farming, vandal—vandalism*:

(a) friend (e) hero
(b) child (f) partner
(c) thief (g) coward
(d) Christian (h) criminal

7. Give the ABSTRACT NOUNS related to these adjectives, e.g.: *strong—strength, timid—timidity*:

(a) proud (c) wise
(b) brave (d) tolerant

(e) broad   (i) kind
(f) clean   (j) scarce
(g) young   (k) anxious
(h) peculiar   (l) poor

NOUNS

Number and Gender

A NOUN referring to **one object** is said to be SINGULAR. A noun referring to **more than one object** is said to be PLURAL, e.g.: *book, books*; *child, children*.

Most nouns form their plural by adding s to the singular.

But: (i) Nouns ending in CH, S, SH, X, add ES, e.g.: *church, churches: bus, buses.*

(ii) Some nouns ending in F or FE change the F or FE into VES, e.g.: *calf, calves*; *knife, knives*; similarly *leaves*; *lives*; *loaves*; *scarves*; *shelves*; *thieves*; *wives*; *wolves*.

(iii) Nouns ending in a consonant + Y change the Y into IES, e.g.: *baby, babies*; *cry, cries*.

(iv) Some nouns ending in O add ES, e.g.: *cargo, cargoes*; similarly *echoes*; *heroes*; *mosquitoes*; *negroes*; *potatoes*; *tomatoes*; *volcanoes*.

(v) Some nouns do not use S at all for their plural, e.g.: *foot, feet*; *child, children*; *man, men*; *woman, women*; *tooth, teeth*; *mouse, mice*; *goose, geese*.

(vi) Some nouns do not change for the plural, e.g.: *sheep*; *deer*; *Swiss*; *Chinese*; *Portuguese*; *aircraft*.

(vii) Some nouns have no plural, e.g.: *information*; *advice*; *news*; *weather*; *knowledge*.

(viii) Some nouns have no singular, e.g.: *police*; *cattle*; *clothes*; *scissors*.

(ix) Compound nouns vary in their plurals, e.g.: *mothers-in-law*; *grown-ups*; *passers-by*; *forget-me-nots*; *women-teachers*; *boy-friends*.

EXERCISES

1. Give the PLURAL of these nouns:

brush, box, handkerchief, shelf, coach, city, class, radio, potato, Burmese, father-in-law.

2. Change these sentences into the SINGULAR:

(a) The sheep grazed in the meadows.
(b) Read the lives of our heroes.
(c) The Japanese built the aircraft.
(d) The flies hovered over the roofs.
(e) The deer wandered along the beaches.

Nouns have four GENDERS:

MASCULINE for males, e.g.: *boy, king, bull.*
FEMININE for females, e.g.: *girl, queen, cow.*
NEUTER if neither masculine nor feminine, e.g.: *desk, sun, table, weight.*
COMMON for either masculine or feminine, e.g.: *baby, person, parent.*

3. Give the FEMININE of:

(a) bull
(b) nephew
(c) actor
(d) bachelor
(e) uncle
(f) landlord
(g) schoolmaster
(h) manager

4. Give the MASCULINE of:

(a) duchess
(b) widow
(c) waitress
(d) heroine
(e) tigress
(f) daughter-in-law
(g) girl-friend
(h) bride

5. Give the GENDER of these nouns:

(a) student
(b) policeman
(c) bicycle
(d) hostess
(e) barmaid
(f) widower
(g) orphan
(h) splinter
(i) subway
(j) pony

24

6. Change all the MASCULINES into the corresponding FEMININES:

(a) The heir to the property was a bachelor.
(b) My great-grandfather was a hero in his boyhood days.
(c) The air-steward handed the money to the bus-conductor.
(d) My nephew was taught Latin by a monk.

7. Give the NUMBER and the GENDER of each of these nouns:

(a) pupil	(f) cow
(b) forget-me-nots	(g) witch
(c) knight	(h) giants
(d) children	(i) musicians
(e) dynamos	(j) aeroplane

LESSON 6

PRONOUNS

Personal, Relative, Possessive

A PRONOUN is a word that **stands for a noun.**
  Look at these sentences:

(a) The girl went home. She did not feel well.
  (*She* is a pronoun because it stands in place of the noun *girl*.)
(b) I spoke to the boy. He had lost his cap.

  (*He* is a pronoun which stands in place of the noun *boy*.)

  The convenience of the PRONOUN is that it enables us to avoid the too frequent repetition of a noun, e.g.:

This house belongs to Mr. Baxter. The house is very spacious. The house is situated in a pleasant district. The house is well built and Mr. Baxter thinks that the house will fetch a high price.

  To avoid using the common noun *house* so often, we employ instead the PRONOUN *it*, e.g.:

This house belongs to Mr. Baxter. *It* is very spacious and has a large garden. *It* is situated in a pleasant district. *It* is well-built and *he* thinks that *it* will fetch a high price.

25

The PRONOUNS *it* and *he* are PERSONAL PRONOUNS.
Others are *them, they, I, we, us, you, him.*

They denote persons or things **without naming them.**

These PERSONAL PRONOUNS stand for THREE PERSONS:

(1) The **first person** or *the person speaking*, e.g.: *I, me, mine, we, ours, us.*

(2) The **second person** signifies *the person or thing spoken to*, e.g.: *you*, and *yours.*

(3) The **third person** is *the person or thing spoken about*, e.g.: *he, him, she, her, it, they.*

The PERSONAL PRONOUNS have a special form to show possession. These are sometimes called POSSESSIVE PRONOUNS, e.g.:

First person: *mine, ours.*

Second person: *thine, yours.*

Third person: *his, hers, theirs.*

A special form of the PERSONAL PRONOUN is used to refer to the noun it replaces, e.g.: *myself, yourself, himself, itself, yourselves, themselves.*

The pronouns *I* and *me* are often incorrectly used and cause confusion, e.g.:

(a) Mother took Jane and I to the circus.
(b) Jane and me went for a ride.

Both of these sentences are wrong and should read:

(a) Mother took Jane and me to the circus.
(b) Jane and I went for a ride.

If we are uncertain whether to use *I* or *me*, we should always try making two little sentences from the one, to test which is correct, e.g.:

Say: Mother took Jane to the circus. Mother took me to the circus.
We are not likely to say: Mother took *I* to the circus.
Say: Jane went for a ride. I went for a ride.
We are not likely to say: *Me* went for a ride.

26

Relative Pronouns

The most important of these are *who, whom, whose, which, what, that.*

They not only take the place of nouns but at the same time join two parts of a sentence. The following illustrates the correct use of the RELATIVE PRONOUN:

The nurse {
who lost her bag has just arrived.
whose bag was lost has just found it.
whom we saw last night is now here.

The bag {
which the nurse lost has been found.
that the nurse lost has been found.

The RELATIVE PRONOUN should always come next to the NOUN to which it relates.

Who, whom, whose, are used for persons.

Which is used for animals and things.

That is used for persons, animals or things, as a defining pronoun.

EXERCISES

1. Write out the following sentences inserting the correct pronouns *I* or *me*.

(a) The new cricket bats were for James and ———.
(b) It is untrue that my friends and ——— were absent.
(c) The play was one which my brother and ——— had seen.
(d) My uncle said that my sister and ——— must share the money.
(e) My aunt sent presents for my brother and ———.

2. Which words in these sentences denote persons or things which are not actually named?

(a) They were not here when I came.
(b) It was not I.
(c) I do not know what you mean.
(d) Are you at home?

(e) Whom did you meet?
(f) Is this your pen?
(g) That is in order.
(h) It was he who did it.
(i) I asked him a question.
(j) He who laughs last, laughs longest.

3. Complete the following sentences with the correct relative pronouns—*who, whose, whom, which, that*:
(a) Is this the cat —— stole the fish?
(b) The man —— lost his way has now returned.
(c) The postman —— bag was lost has just found it.
(d) I never knew —— to choose.
(e) This is the house —— Jack built.

4. Complete correctly these sentences using:

in whom, to whom, from whom, upon whom, with whom—
(a) The friends —— Rip Van Winkle associated were all dead.
(b) My friend, —— I trusted, has betrayed me.
(c) He is the man —— I received the award.
(d) The Prime Minister is the man —— all responsibility rests.
(e) The man —— I looked for help has failed me.

In modern English it is quite acceptable to put the preposition later in the sentence, e.g.:

The man *to whom* I was speaking is my brother.
The man *whom* I was speaking *to* is my brother.

5. Do Exercise 4 again, putting the prepositions later in the sentences.

6. Complete these sentences with *in whose, from whose, to whose, upon whose, with whose*:
(a) My sister, —— friends I was staying, went to Devon.
(b) He is the surgeon —— hands I placed my life.
(c) The man —— shoulders the burden of responsibility fell was murdered.

28

(d) The dentist —— surgery I was directed was not in.

(e) The man —— shop the articles were stolen reported the matter to the police.

LESSON 7

PRONOUNS

Interrogative, Demonstrative, Indefinite

Besides PERSONAL, RELATIVE, and POSSESSIVE PRONOUNS there are also INTERROGATIVE, DEMONSTRATIVE, and INDEFINITE PRONOUNS.

Interrogative Pronouns are used when we are **asking questions,** and the chief pronouns of this type are *who?*, *which?*, *whom?*, *whose?*, *what?*

They must introduce questions and are not accompanied by nouns, e.g.:

"Who is it?"

"Which will you choose?"

"Whose is this pen?"

"What did you say?"

"To whom did it belong?" *or* "Whom did it belong to?"

Demonstrative Pronouns are those which **point out** or **distinguish things.** If they are accompanied by a noun, they are no longer pronouns, but "pointing out" or demonstrative ADJECTIVES.

The chief DEMONSTRATIVE PRONOUNS are *this* and *that*, with their plural forms *these* and *those*; *such* and *same*.

Examples
This is wrong.
What is *that*?
These are better than *those*.
She is really a truthful girl, although she does not behave as *such*.
I asked the next boy but he told me the *same*.

Now look at the next examples:
This book was lost.
These friends were absent.
That boy was present.
He gave me *such* a fright.
The *same* thing happened.

The words in italics are "pointing out" ADJECTIVES, as in each case they "point out" the noun, e.g., in the first example, *this* book—*this* points out the *book*.

Indefinite Pronouns. Some pronouns refer to things in a vague and indefinite way. They do not stand for any definite noun. The chief are:
any, anything, anybody, some, something, somebody, none, nothing, nobody, all, each, etc.
Again we must be careful to distinguish these words when used to describe nouns, e.g., He took *some* sugar. Here *some* is an indefinite ADJECTIVE of quantity because it refers to the noun *sugar*.

Examples of INDEFINITE PRONOUNS:

I have not spoken to *anybody*.
Anything can happen.
Anyone could have done it.
Many are called but *few* are chosen.
One feels sorry for him.

EXERCISES

1. What kind of PRONOUNS are the words in italics? Remember that they may be PERSONAL, RELATIVE, etc., as well as the three kinds mentioned in this chapter:

(a) As *I* was unable to walk, *we* went by train.
(b) *Nobody* went to the party.
(c) *What* do *you* want?
(d) *This* is the house *that* Jack built.
(e) The man to *whom I* was speaking was a detective.
(f) *Someone* has been eating my porridge.
(g) *Anybody* could do *this*.
(h) *What* do *you* think you are doing?
(i) *Thine* is the kingdom.
(j) *That* is *mine*.

2. From the following list of INTERROGATIVE PRONOUNS place the most suitable in the questions given below—*what, whom, which, who, whose*:

(a) —— way did he go?
(b) Halt! —— goes there?
(c) — is this cat?
(d) To —— did you give the book?
(e) — is the date today?
(f) —— did this?
(g) —— are you going to do about it?

Remember that the words *this, that, these* and *those* are DEMONSTRATIVE ADJECTIVES when they are used before a noun, e.g., I like *these* pears, or I will take *this* loaf, but when they are used alone they are DEMONSTRATIVE PRONOUNS, e.g., I will take *this*, or I like *these*.

3. In the following sentences state whether the words in italics are "pointing out" ADJECTIVES or "pointing out" PRONOUNS:

(a) *These* belong to me.
(b) *Those* flowers are very beautiful.
(c) *That* boy has done wrong.
(d) *That* is wrong.
(e) *This* is the right way.
(f) *This* way is right.
(g) *These* pears are unripe.
(h) *These* shoes are cheaper than *those*.

In the same way the words *which, what* and *whose* are INTERROGATIVE ADJECTIVES when used with a noun and when they ask a question, but they are INTERROGATIVE PRONOUNS when used alone, e.g.:

What is the next lesson? (Interrogative Pronoun)
What lesson comes next? (Interrogative Adjective)
Which is the correct way to do this? (Interrogative Pronoun)
Which way is correct? (Interrogative Adjective)

4. In the following sentences state whether the words in italics are INTERROGATIVE PRONOUNS or INTERROGATIVE ADJECTIVES:
(a) *What* are you going to do about it?
(b) *What* decision did you reach?
(c) *Which* is the way to school?
(d) *Which* road leads to the school?
(e) *Whose* cap is this?
(f) *Whose* is this?
(g) *What* game do you like best?
(h) *What* is today's date?

5. State which words are INDEFINITE PRONOUNS or INDEFINITE ADJECTIVES. Remember that the word is an INDEFINITE PRONOUN if used alone and an INDEFINITE ADJECTIVE OF QUANTITY if used with a noun.
(a) *All* people that on earth do dwell.
(b) *Some* were pleased but a *few* were angry.
(c) The refugees were given *some* soup.
(d) *One* could not help but feel sorry for him.
(e) Has *anything* unusual happened?
(f) *Someone* has stolen my watch.
(g) I have *no* sugar in my tea.
(h) *Anyone* could have done this.

ADJECTIVES

Demonstrative, Possessive, Quality, Quantity, Interrogative

An ADJECTIVE is a word **used to add something to the meaning of a** NOUN **or** PRONOUN and so to restrict or limit its meaning, e.g.:

A *beautiful* flower. A *large* fish. *Five* men remain.

Adjectives help us to describe persons, places, or things, and in a sense may be said to supply the "clothing" of NOUNS. ADJECTIVES are put into various classes:

Demonstrative

As we have already seen, DEMONSTRATIVE ADJECTIVES are used **before** a NOUN and point out. They answer the question *which?*, e.g.:

That chair. *This* picture. He came from *that* town.

Possessive

These are closely connected with the former, e.g.:
My friend. *Our* garden. *Your* face. *His* bicycle. *Their* home.

Quality

These tell what *sort* or *kind*, e.g.:

The soldier wore a *heavy* coat.
There was a *keen* wind blowing.

Quantity or Number

These tell how many or how *much*, e.g.:

There were *three* cups.
He drank *some* water.
Few people were present.

All numbers when used with nouns are ADJECTIVES OF QUANTITY and so are words expressing an indefinite quantity, such as *some, few, several, enough,* etc.

Interrogative Adjectives must be used with a noun and merely ask a question, e.g.:

Which way did he go?
What answer did he give?

EXERCISES

1. Write down the ADJECTIVES in the following sentences:
(a) John is a clumsy boy.
(b) Did you bring a clean handkerchief?
(c) Fetch me the green book which is on the table.
(d) She bought a blue dress.
(e) We have never seen such a magnificent sight.
(f) The vivid lightning dazzled our eyes.
(g) I can recommend this exciting story.
(h) Many people watched the game.

2. Read again how adjectives are classified and state the *kind* of each ADJECTIVE in italics in the following sentences:
(a) *Which* subject do you like best at school?
(b) I should not like to live in *that* district.
(c) It was *heavy* rain.
(d) *Her* father was ill.
(e) There are *ten* boys absent today.
(f) *Each* child was given a piece of cake.
(g) He had *no* ice-cream left.
(h) There was a *sudden* pause.
(i) *Our* house is in the country.
(j) *Which* turning did he take?

34

3. On the left-hand side there are eight ADJECTIVES; on the right are eight NOUNS. Add to each noun the most suitable adjective:

ADJECTIVES	NOUNS
juicy	building
woollen	child
shallow	hillside
urgent	jacket
overcast	message
deaf	orange
square	river
steep	sky

4. Choose two of the ADJECTIVES on the right to describe suitably each NOUN on the left:

(a) TRAIN   (hard, fast, wicked, hairy, electric)
(b) HORSE   (black, endless, square, big, blue)
(c) OCCASION (pink, suitable, wide, sad, silvery)
(d) UMBRELLA (kind, clever, useful, new, yellow)
(e) POND   (filthy, deep, woollen, small, old)

5. Add ADJECTIVES opposite in meaning to those in italics:

(a) The doctor was not *rough* with the child; he was quite ——.
(b) One criminal was *little-known*; the other was ——.
(c) Those are not the *even* numbers; they are the —— numbers.
(d) The *priceless* articles are at the back of the shop; the —— ones are at the front.
(e) One fellow was *bearded*; the other was ——.

As we have seen, INTERROGATIVE ADJECTIVES ask a question. The three words *which?*, *what?* and *whose?* are interrogative adjectives **if they are used with a noun when asking a question,** but are INTERROGATIVE PRONOUNS **if used alone,** e.g.:

What did you do? (Interrogative pronoun)
What occupation did he follow? (Interrogative adjective)
Whose is this? (Interrogative pronoun)
Whose cap is this? (Interrogative adjective)

6. State whether the words in italics in the following sentences are INTERROGATIVE ADJECTIVES or INTERROGATIVE PRONOUNS:

(a) *Which* is the tallest?
(b) *Which* pear is the juiciest?
(c) *Whose* satchel is this?
(d) *Whose* are these aprons?
(e) *What* can you do to help?
(f) *Which* do you prefer?
(g) *What* kind of animal is that?
(h) *Whose* story can I believe?

LESSON 9

THE ARTICLES

Comparison of Adjectives

A and *an* are called the INDEFINITE ARTICLES as they **point out no special person or thing.**

The is the DEFINITE ARTICLE as it **refers to some special person or thing.**

As a general rule, *an* is used before NOUNS which begin with one of the VOWELS—a, e, i, o and u—e.g.:

An apple, *an* egg, *an* island, *an* owl, *an* uncle, etc.

Sometimes it sounds better to use *a* before a word beginning with *u* having the sound of *y*, e.g.:

A university, *a* unit, *a* uniform.

Where the word begins with *y* itself, and has the sound of *u*, we use *a*, e.g., *a* youth, *a* young man, etc.

In most other cases *a* is used before NOUNS beginning with a CONSONANT, e.g.:

A box, *a* cup, *a* classroom, etc.

In some cases where *h* is not sounded, we use *an*, e.g.:
An hour; *an* honest man; Brutus is *an* honourable man.

EXERCISES

1. Write out in your exercise books the following sentences, filling in the blanks with *a* or *an* as the case may be.
(a) The hen laid —— egg.
(b) The train was —— hour late.
(c) The patient was conveyed to —— hospital in —— ambulance.
(d) In his dream he thought he saw —— unicorn.
(e) —— ostrich and —— vulture are both large birds.
(f) He was only —— youth, but he became —— heir to —— estate.
(g) The winning of —— scholarship to —— university is —— honourable achievement.
(h) —— minute is —— unit of time.
(i) The girl brought —— orange and —— apple to school.
(j) He lost —— umbrella and —— overcoat.

Comparison of Adjectives

Describing words vary in degree, e.g.:

A *big* boy; A *bigger* boy; The *biggest* boy.

In this case there must be three or more boys to make the comparison. It is wrong to say *the biggest boy* when only two are being compared.

Most adjectives are compared in this way, but we can also use the words MORE and MOST to express degree in many cases, e.g.:

beautiful	more beautiful	most beautiful
or, wonderful	more wonderful	most wonderful

37

The degrees of comparison are called POSITIVE, COMPARATIVE and SUPERLATIVE, e.g.:

POSITIVE	COMPARATIVE	SUPERLATIVE
tall	taller	tallest
slow	slower	slowest

Note especially: We must not use the expression *more taller* as this is a "double comparative", or *most tallest* as this is a "double superlative", and incorrect English.

There are certain adjectives which cannot be compared in either of these ways. We should learn the following:

POSITIVE	COMPARATIVE	SUPERLATIVE
good	better	best
bad	worse	worst
much (many)	more	most
little	less	least
late	later (latter)	latest (last)
near	nearer	nearest (next)
old	older (elder)	oldest (eldest)

There are certain adjectives which cannot be compared, such as *each, this, third,* etc., and adjectives such as *golden, unique, square,* and *perfect.* For example, *a perfect sight* cannot be *more* or *less* perfect, nor can an object be *more square* than *square.* You should also remember that *fewer* is used for numbers that can be divided, as in *fewer volumes,* but *less* is used for quantity and size, as in *less* work.

2. Write complete sentences by using the correct form of the ADJECTIVE which is given on the left-hand side:

(a) SHORT   She was the —— of the two girls.
(b) UGLY   This hat is ugly but that one is ——.
(c) FINE   This scenery is the —— in the world.
(d) THIN   He was the —— boy in the class.
(e) LESS   He did not know the —— thing about it.
(f) PROUD   I am —— of you than I am of your brother.
(g) GENTLE   She was the —— girl of them all.
(h) OLD   I am —— than you.

3. Give the SUPERLATIVE degree of the following adjectives:

(a) bad (b) little (c) near (d) square

Give the COMPARATIVE degree of:

(e) great (f) old (g) pretty (h) few (i) ill

Give the POSITIVE form of the following:

(j) freer (k) fastest (l) latest (m) least (n) nearer

4. Form ADJECTIVES from these NOUNS:

> e.g.: *thunder—thundery*
> *fortune—fortunate*

(a) rain   (e) courtesy
(b) anxiety   (f) beauty
(c) strength   (g) gratitude
(d) pride   (h) solitude

5. Form ABSTRACT NOUNS from these ADJECTIVES:

> e.g.: *wide—width*
> *hungry—hunger*

(a) modest   (e) happy
(b) honest   (f) comfortable
(c) brave   (g) glorious
(d) sad   (d) joyous

LESSON 10

VERBS

Transitive and Intransitive, Active and Passive, Auxiliary

A VERB is usually described as a *being, doing, having, saying,* or *thinking* word.

It is derived from the Latin *verbum* (= word).

No sentence is really complete without a VERB.

When any "subject" is mentioned, something must be said about it in the PREDICATE.

The VERB is the chief part of the PREDICATE, as we see in the following sentences where only the VERB is in italics:

The horse *eats* hay. Cows *chew* the cud. The boy *ran* home.

A VERB is said to be TRANSITIVE **when it needs an** OBJECT **to make complete sense, e.g.:**

He broke a *window*. (object)

An INTRANSITIVE VERB makes a complete statement and **does not require an object, e.g.:**

The bird sings. The fire burns.

TRANSITIVE VERBS may be:

(a) ACTIVE, where the subject performs the action, e.g.:
The horse drinks water.

(b) PASSIVE, when the subject has the action done to it, e.g.:
Water is drunk by the horse.

ACTIVE: He taught me French.
PASSIVE: I was taught French by him.

A VERB sometimes consists of more than one word, e.g.:

She *has* broken her arm.	The two little words in italics are
I *am* going home.	AUXILIARY VERBS.

The chief AUXILIARY, or helping, verbs are TO BE and TO HAVE. In learning a foreign language such as French, it is usual to learn them first, and in English they are equally important.

The simple present TENSES (see page 43) of the two chief AUXILIARY VERBS are as follows:

TO BE

PRESENT TENSE (or time)

I am		We are	
Thou art	Singular	You are	Plural
He (she) is		They are	

TO HAVE

PRESENT TENSE (or time)

I have			We have	
Thou hast	} Singular		You have	} Plural
He (she) has			They have	

We can work out for ourselves the other tenses of these verbs:

FUTURE I shall be   FUTURE I shall have

PAST I was   PAST I had

EXERCISES

1. The VERBS are missing from the following sentences; find
   them from this list and then write the complete sentences:
laugh, jump, seized, fasten, practise, push, doze, doubt, drain,
swing, knock.

(a) The boys liked to —— on the gate.

(b) Most rivers —— into the sea.

(c) It is dangerous to —— one another on the stairs.

(d) Do not let the cat —— on the table.

(e) The cat will —— in front of the fire.

(f) Do not —— at me.

(g) He did not —— at the door.

(h) The criminals were —— by the police.

(i) The girl did not —— on the piano.

(j) I do not —— your word.

(k) The boy could not —— his shoe lace.

2. Write the verbs of these sentences in two columns, TRANSI-
   TIVE and INTRANSITIVE:

(a) The girl wept.

(b) The dog stole a large piece of meat.

(c) My daughter begins work next month.

(d) The sun shone brightly.

41

(e) The pupils learn grammar.

(f) The school closed at 4 p.m.

(g) The boys jumped the stream.

(h) The sheep graze in the fields.

3. Change the verbs of these sentences from ACTIVE to PASSIVE:

> e.g. The cat caught the mouse. (ACTIVE)
> The mouse was caught by the cat. (PASSIVE)

(a) The conjurer performed several new tricks.

(b) The new porter will ring the bell today.

(c) The explosion shattered the windows.

(d) A ferocious dog bit me.

(e) A gang of young thieves stole the apples.

(f) She knitted a pair of socks.

(g) Mr. Smith rarely visits the doctor.

(h) The floods caused a great deal of damage to the crops.

4. Now change these sentences so that the verb is ACTIVE instead of PASSIVE:

(a) The fruit was eaten by the girls.

(b) The ball was caught by the wicket-keeper.

(c) The boys were trapped by the incoming tide.

(d) The train was delayed by a thick fog.

(e) The match was witnessed by a large crowd of spectators.

(f) The people were terrified by the advance of the enemy.

(g) The stolen car had been abandoned by the thieves.

(h) Very pretty dresses were worn by the bridesmaids.

5. Change the following sentences by using an AUXILIARY VERB with the main verb, e.g.:

The hunter shot the wolf.

The hunter *had* shot the wolf.

(a) He broke his ankle.

(b) He arrived at school in good time.

(c) We flew to Austria for our holiday.

(d) You came too late to be of any assistance.
(e) Blériot flew across the English Channel in 1909.
(f) We talked far into the night.
(g) I lose my way in the dark wood.

LESSON 11

VERBS

Mood, Tense, Number, Person, Infinitive, Participles

VERBS have what is known as MOOD, TENSE, NUMBER, and PERSON.

The word MOOD, which comes from the Latin *modus* (= manner), denotes the way in which the statement is made.

The INDICATIVE MOOD **makes a statement or asks a question,** e.g.:

I have brought my umbrella. Will it rain?

The IMPERATIVE MOOD **expresses a command or a request,** e.g.:

Stop. Please shut the door.

The SUBJUNCTIVE MOOD is used in expressing certain conditions or wishes or doubts, e.g.:

If I were you, I should wear an overcoat.
I wish it were true.
I demand that it be done.

VERBS have TENSES. The word comes from the Latin *tempus* (= time).

The three main tenses of verbs are:

The PRESENT TENSE: It rains *or* It is raining.
The PAST TENSE: It rained *or* It was raining.
THE FUTURE TENSE: It will rain *or* It will be raining.

43

What are called the PRINCIPAL PARTS of a verb are:

The PRESENT TENSE   e.g.: I write
    PAST TENSE   e.g.: I wrote
    PAST PARTICIPLE   e.g.: written
    PRESENT PARTICIPLE   e.g.: writing

A special verb-part, which usually has *to* in front of it, is known as the INFINITIVE, e.g.: *to walk, to belong, to read.*

Verbs also have SINGULAR and PLURAL NUMBERS, and three PERSONS for the singular and three PERSONS for the plural.

Here are the six persons of the Present Indicative of the verb *to run*:

FIRST PERSON SINGULAR	I run
SECOND PERSON SINGULAR	you run
THIRD PERSON SINGULAR	he or she or it runs
FIRST PERSON PLURAL	we run
SECOND PERSON PLURAL	you run
THIRD PERSON PLURAL	they run

Most verbs form their PAST TENSE and PAST PARTICIPLE by adding "d" or "ed", e.g.: "smile—smiled"; "paint—painted".

But many verbs have irregular Past Tenses and Past Participles. Here are a few:

beseech, besought, besought
bid (= tell), bade, bidden
bid (= offer money), bid, bid
bind, bound, bound
bite, bit, bitten
choose, chose, chosen
creep, crept, crept
deal, dealt, dealt
dwell, dwelt, dwelt
fly, flew, flown

freeze, froze, frozen
lay, laid, laid
lie (= be flat), lay, lain
pay, paid, paid
rise, rose, risen
seek, sought, sought
swear, swore, sworn
tread, trod, trodden
drink, drank, drunk
spin, span, spun

EXERCISES

1. Change the PRESENT TENSES into PAST TENSES:

(a) He pulls his chair up to the window, sits down, and stays there for two hours.
(b) The shop-girl stands behind the counter all day.
(c) When I say I dream I can fly, I mean "fly with wings", not "fly in a plane".
(d) The dog bites him as soon as he treads on its tail.
(e) They swear that they know his name and that they recognize him.
(f) The car strikes her; she falls, and lies unconscious on the ground.
(g) She lays her coat over the sleeping baby.
(h) They cost less money when I buy them by the dozen.

2. What is the TENSE of the verb in each sentence?

(a) I shall return to London.
(b) He arrived home last night.
(c) I am doing my homework.
(d) I shall be coming to see you tomorrow.
(e) I skated on the pond.

3. Give the MOOD of these verbs:

(a) My mother baked a cake.
(b) If I were you, I should not hesitate.
(c) Come in and shut the door.
(d) I do not like arithmetic.
(e) I wish I could go home.

4. Give the PERSON and NUMBER of the verbs in these sentences:

e.g.: She is sewing—THIRD PERSON SINGULAR.

(a) They were running along the towpath.
(b) I am not going to wait any longer.
(c) We laugh when we are amused.

(d) Jane, you must not cross the road without looking.

(e) Boys, fall in line.

(f) He who laughs last laughs longest.

(g) Be quiet, girls.

(h) They were all talking at once.

The Participles

The PRESENT PARTICIPLE—"writing". Present Participles end in ING. When the verb ends in E, this final E is usually dropped before ING, e.g., "move"—PRESENT PARTICIPLE "moving".

Uses of PRESENT PARTICIPLE:

(a) As an adjective—"a galloping horse".

(b) Beginning certain adjectival phrases—"Round the head-land, the ship went out of sight". Such participial phrases must be related to the subject of the main verb of the sentence. If we say, "*Getting into the car*, the tyre burst", the phrase is not related to "the tyre" because the tyre did not get into the car. It is better to say, "As we were getting into the car, the tyre burst."

The PAST PARTICIPLE ends in ED, T, or EN: crept, killed, beaten, etc. Sometimes it is the same as the PAST TENSE, e.g.:

I *settled* the account. (past tense of verb "settle")

The account was *settled*. (past participle)

Sometimes it is different and is often confused with the past tense, e.g., "I done my homework in one hour." This is the wrong use of the past participle. The sentence should be, "I *did* my homework in one hour." (past tense). See also p. 52.

5. Use the correct form of the verb in the brackets to complete these sentences:

(a) He was —— in the bus. (sat, sitting)

(b) The boy was —— on the pavement. (stood, standing)

(c) The money was —— in the drawer. (hid, hidden)

(d) The coat was seen —— in the wardrobe. (hung, hanging)
(e) The weary tramp was —— on the grass. (laid, lying)
(f) I —— nothing to you. (did, done)

LESSON 12

REVISION TEST (1)

A.1. State the kind of NOUN each of the following is:

January	crew	sculptor	coinage
Saturday	honesty	throne	flower
regiment	Gillian	Easter	cousin
patience	Taylor	crowd	uncle
table	tailor	teacher	hydrogen
Table Bay	swarm	Christ	Byron
choir	mercy	Africa	music
year	coal	queen	pity
aeroplane	cottage	England	harbour
stream	stable	Matthew	fleet

2. Write down the verbs which can be formed from these nouns:

(a) sadness
(b) courage
(c) trust
(d) simplicity
(e) decision
(f) cleanliness
(g) advice
(h) necessity
(i) solution
(j) darkness

3. Give a single word for each of these:

(a) A man whose wife is dead.
(b) A person who never eats meat.
(c) A man who writes books.
(d) A woman who does a very brave deed.
(e) A person who makes bread.

(f) A woman who looks after the passengers in a plane.
(g) A person who is always hopeful and is sure everything will
be all right.
(h) A person who is passing when something happens.

4. What COLLECTIVE NOUN do we use when we refer to a
number of the following?

(a) cows
(b) footballers
(c) sheep
(d) stairs

(e) fish
(f) trees
(g) military musicians

B.1. Rewrite these sentences correctly:
(a) The table was sold to an old lady with carved oak legs.
(b) A party will be given for the children of all soldiers below
the age of ten.
(c) He is the tallest of the twins.
(d) I can draw more better than you.
(e) He learns me arithmetic.
(f) While reading his newspaper his train arrived.
(g) I gave him everything what he would need.
(h) Cook the fish slowly while simmering in hot water.

2. Form NOUNS from the following VERBS:

(a) laugh
(b) introduce
(c) spend

(d) produce
(e) punish
(f) sell

3. Form ADJECTIVES from the following NOUNS:

(a) thunder
(b) winter
(c) grief

(d) breadth
(e) anxiety
(f) charm

4. Give the TENSE, NUMBER and PERSON of the VERBS in the
following sentences:

(a) He will return to Manchester.

(b) I am learning to swim.
(c) We went for a long walk through the woods.
(d) "Will you be going to the dance tomorrow, Jane?"
(e) She asked the girls if they had been to the dance.

C.1. What PART OF SPEECH is each of the words in italics?

(a) He was a *fast* swimmer.
(b) People often *fast* during Lent.
(c) Do not drive too *fast*.
(d) He broke his *fast* after ten days.
(e) Will you come *round* to my house?
(f) The world is *round* in shape.
(g) Please will you *round* off the show with a song?
(h) They sang the *round* called "Three Blind Mice".
(i) She remained *behind*.
(j) It was *behind* the door all the time.

2. In what MOOD are the VERBS in italics in these sentences?

(a) I *am going* to the cinema tonight.
(b) If I *were* you I should not go to the cinema tonight.
(c) *May you be* happy after all you have suffered.
(d) *Give him* the book.
(e) *Go* at once before it is too late.

3. Write out the following sentences by using the correct form
   of the ADJECTIVE given on the left-hand side.

(a) DRY   March was the —— month of the year.
(b) DEEP   This pond is the —— of the two.
(c) FASCINATING She was the —— of the two girls.
(d) FAST   Which of the two boys is the —— swim-
                 mer?
(e) MILD   It was the —— soap of all.
(f) WISE   He was the —— boy among them.
(g) UPPER   He had reached the —— limit.
(h) SHORT   There are two roads leading to the cottage
                 but this one is the ——.

4. Complete each of the following sentences by putting in the blank spaces the correct PRONOUN from the brackets.

(a) (He, him), and (I, me) went to the cinema.
(b) (These, them) are not fit to eat.
(c) She told me that they did it (theirselves, themselves, themself).
(d) Will you lend (I, me) your pencil?
(e) For (who, whom) are you working?

5. From the following list of INTERROGATIVE PRONOUNS place the most suitable in the questions:

What? whom? which? who? whose?—

(a) —— is the best way?
(b) —— are you going to do?
(c) —— cat is this?
(d) Halt! —— goes there?
(e) For —— is the bell tolling?

LESSON 13

SPECIAL FORMS OF VERBS

As we have seen, the verb "TO BE" and the verb "TO HAVE" are sometimes classed as "AUXILIARY" or "helping out" verbs. Their various numbers are often confused. When we speak of ONE it is SINGULAR and *IS* should be used.

When we speak of MORE THAN ONE it is PLURAL and *ARE* should be used, e.g.:

Neither (one) is here. (singular)
Both are here. (plural)

EXERCISES

1. Write out the following sentences with the correct form of the verb *to be*.

(a) Each of the books (is, are) mine.
(b) There (was, were) only one girl in the room.
(c) (Was, were) you there?
(d) A pretty green and yellow frock (is, are) in the window.
(e) Both of the pencils (is, are) mine.
(f) A white tulip and a red one (was, were) in the vase.

HAS and *HAVE* often cause confusion.
HAS is SINGULAR and refers to ONE only.
HAVE is PLURAL and refers to SEVERAL.

2. Write out the following sentences using the word *has* or *have*:

(a) Neither the boy nor the girl (has, have) gone to school.
(b) Either the cat or the dog (has, have) stolen the meat.
(c) Many of them (has, have) disappeared.
(d) A box of pencils and crayons (has, have) been lost.
(e) All of them (has, have) gone to the playing field.
(f) Every one of them (has, have) come back.

Sometimes the verb *have* when used with another verb means to cause or to give effect to—as in the following examples:
    to have made; to have printed; to have destroyed;
    "The chief said that he would have the hut destroyed."
This means that *he would get someone else* to destroy it.
    Now say what is the difference between:
    I have dug my garden *and* I had my garden dug.

The verbs *to lie* and *to lay*
    These verbs are often confused. The correct forms are:
(a) To lie down (lie, lying, lay, lain), e.g.: I lie down.

51

(b) To lay a thing down (lay, laying, laid), e.g.: I lay down my pen.

(c) To (lie, lying, lied) (to tell an untruth), e.g.: You lie to me.

The verb *to lie* is **intransitive**—that is, it does not take an object.

The verb *to lay* is **transitive** and is followed by an object.

3. Complete the following sentences using the correct form of the verb *lie* or *lay*.

(a) The farmer —— in wait for the fox.
(b) The hen —— a brown egg.
(c) The thief had to —— low for a time.
(d) The rebels —— down their arms.
(e) The boy has —— to the master.
(f) The maid —— the table very quickly.
(g) Let sleeping dogs ——.
(h) Can you —— a trail?

The word *do* and its past participle *done* are among the most used words in the English language. Not only is this verb used as an auxiliary with other verbs, e.g.: *I didn't go*; *They do have*; *We don't think*; but it is also used in hundreds of different idioms which cannot be explained grammatically. This common reliance on the verb *do* tends to make people lazy in their expression and they sometimes use it wrongly.

Example: Transport is done by roads. (Wrong)
    Transport is by road. (Correct)

In the above sentence *transport* is an **abstract noun.** One cannot "do" transport. It is correct, however, to say:

Ploughing is done by tractor.
Weaving is done by hand.

People often make mistakes about *DID* and *DONE*. To say, "I done it" is wrong. The correct form is "I did it". *DONE* cannot be used by itself as a verb; some other word such as *is* or *have* is used with it, e.g.: It is done, *or* I have done.

4. Write out the following sentences using either *did* or *done*.

(a) I —— the exercise you gave me to do.
(b) The girl —— her homework and then went out to play.
(c) Have you —— it yet?
(d) She has never —— it before.
(e) She said she —— not know what was the matter.
(f) The work has not been —— correctly.
(g) Well ——! I am very proud of you.

The verb *SEE*

This needs care, especially in the forms *saw* and *seen*. People often say "I seen him" when they really mean to say, "I saw him".

SAW is past tense, whereas SEEN is a past participle. *Seen* cannot be used by itself as a verb; some other word such as *is* or *have* must be used with it.

5. Write out the following sentences with the correct form of the verb "see":

(a) Please will you —— to it?
(b) The girls have —— us.
(c) He has not —— me today.
(d) Did you —— what I ——?
(e) We have —— something which we never —— before.
(f) My suit has —— better days.

CAN and MAY

"I *can* do this" really means, " I *am able* to do this".
"*May* I do this?" asks permission.
"*Can* I do this?" means, "Am I able to do this?"
"I *may* do this" expresses doubt, as we may or may not do something, OR it shows that permission has been granted, e.g.: "I may come" (am allowed to).

Note: In the PAST TENSE *can* becomes *could* and *may* becomes *might*.

6. Rewrite these sentences, using "can" or "may" according to the sense:

(a) —— I be excused from attending prayers? (asking permission)

(b) Perhaps I —— go to the dance tonight.

(c) —— you swim two lengths of the pool yet?

(d) You —— go home if you wish.

(e) My mother says that I —— stay out till 9 p.m.

(f) I —— come to tea, but I —— not stay later than 8 p.m.

SHALL and *WILL*.

We use the words *shall* and *will* with verbs to show the future.

SINGULAR	PLURAL
I shall come tomorrow.	We shall come tomorrow.
You will come tomorrow.	You will come tomorrow.
He She will come tomorrow.	They will come tomorrow.

7. Re-write these sentences in the FUTURE TENSE:

(a) I come to school on the bus.

(b) She arrives early.

(c) We begin school on Monday next.

(d) He assists me in the shop.

(e) They frighten me in the dark.

(f) Do I get an answer soon?

If we want to express not just simple futurity, but strong determination or threat or refusal, we use WILL for 'I' and 'we' and SHALL for other persons, for example:

"I *will* marry him. You *shall* not stop me," the girl declared resolutely.

54

8. Re-write these sentences, using SHALL and WILL correctly:

(a) "They —— pay back every penny, the swindlers," swore the angry old man.

(b) "I —— come whatever happens," he declared stubbornly.

(c) "We —— go there with or without you" I insisted.

(d) "He —— never come here again," I shouted emphatically.

(e) "I —— love you for ever," the young man promised.

WILL is used more and more in modern English with 'I' and 'we' for simple futurity (as well as determination or refusal), though SHALL is still always used in questions with 'I' and 'we', for example:

> Father: "Who will be coming with me tomorrow?"
> George: "I will. It's my turn. Shall I bring my raincoat with me?"

SHOULD and WOULD

When we want to say that something may possibly happen, or is likely to occur in certain conditions we need a different tense from the straightforward future tense. We need the CONDITIONAL TENSE. Instead of *shall* and *will* we say *should* and *would.*

Should is used in much the same way as *shall*, e.g.:

I *should* not be happy with that arrangement.

Would is used in much the same way as *will*, e.g.:

He *would* move to London if he could.

Remember also that verbs such as *prefer, be glad, like,* which have an idea of "hope" or "wishing" are used with *should* and *would*, e.g.:

They would prefer to hold the concert in the evening.

Sentences expressing actions that were frequent or a habit also take *would*:

We would go to the market place every day.

Another use of *should* is to express duty, e.g.:

Every Member of Parliament should attend these meetings.

LESSON 14

ADVERBS

Classes

An ADVERB is a word which **modifies** or **limits** a verb, an adjective, another adverb, a preposition or a conjunction.

1. ADVERBS of MANNER **answer the question "how?"**, e.g.:
swiftly, rapidly, slowly, easily, etc.
"The goalkeeper ran swiftly towards the ball." *Swiftly* tells how he ran.

2. ADVERBS of TIME **answer the question "when?"**, e.g.:
now, then, soon, lately, always, presently, etc.
"She will be going soon." *Soon* tells when she is going.

3. ADVERBS of PLACE **answer the question "where?"**, e.g.:
here, there, where, below, near, etc.
"They are not here." *Here* is in reply to the question "where?"

4. ADVERBS of DEGREE **answer the question "To what extent?"**
    e.g.:
nearly, very, much, scarcely, etc.
"I was *nearly* knocked down by the car."

NOTE: The same word may be either an adjective or an adverb.
A *fast* car. *Fast* is an adjective because it describes the NOUN
car.
He ran *fast*. *Fast* is an adverb because it describes the verb *ran*.
The *early* bird catches the worm. *Early* is an adjective because
it describes the NOUN *bird*.
He arrived *early*. Here *early* is an adverb as it is added to the
verb *arrived*.

Here is a little table of words which are usually ADVERBS.
This list is by no means complete but it may help you in the
following exercises.

ADVERBS OF MANNER	ADVERBS OF TIME	ADVERBS OF PLACE	ADVERBS OF DEGREE
carefully	seldom	under	quite
boldly	weekly	over	too
heavily	yearly	above	very
famously	annually	below	much
brightly	often	here	more
cheerfully	since	there	mostly
neatly	rarely	everywhere	greatly
hungrily	yesterday	within	tremendously
coldly	early	without	rather
truly	tomorrow	beyond	nearly
faithfully	repeatedly	far	almost
honestly	immediately	anywhere	sufficiently

EXERCISES

1. State whether the words in italics are ADJECTIVES or
   ADVERBS:
(a) If you work *hard* you will succeed.
(b) This was a *hard* case.
(c) She rose *early* in the morning.
(d) I caught an *early* train.

(e) He leadeth me beside the *still* waters.

(f) He will *still* remain my friend.

(g) Their prospects were *most* favourable.

(h) He accepted *most* gladly.

(i) It was an *easy* victory.

(j) The sergeant said, "Stand *easy*."

(k) The prisoner had a *fair* trial.

(l) He did not play *fair*.

(m) The earth revolves *round* the sun.

(n) He was a long time coming *round*.

(o) It was *round* about Christmas time.

(p) It was a *round* object.

2. In the following sentences write out the ADVERBS of MANNER:

(a) Slowly and sadly we laid him down.

(b) He behaved nobly.

(c) The river flows swiftly.

(d) The fireman was severely injured.

3. Now write down the ADVERBS of TIME:

(a) It was a fine day yesterday.

(b) I have not seen you lately.

(c) Where have you been recently?

(d) I can seldom remember his birthday.

4. Write down the ADVERBS of PLACE:

(a) Captain! art thou sleeping there below?

(b) We must stay indoors today.

(c) Will you come here?

(d) She ran hither and thither.

5. Write down the ADVERBS of DEGREE:

(a) He was almost at the end of his tether.

(b) I am quite well, thank you.

(c) You have not been sufficiently careful.

(d) He went too far.

6. State the CLASS to which each of the following ADVERBS belongs:

(a) tomorrow (d) entirely (g) fiercely (j) too
(b) early (e) happily (h) often (k) long since
(c) fatally (f) within (i) very (l) there

7. Rewrite these sentences adding the most suitable ADVERB from this list:

peacefully, recklessly, ferociously, gracefully, greedily, slowly, gratefully, severely, sweetly, abruptly.

(a) She accepted the gift ——. (f) The dog barked ——.
(b) He was punished ——. (g) She danced ——.
(c) The baby slept ——. (h) She stopped ——.
(d) The old lady walked ——. (i) The boy ate ——.
(e) The motorist drove ——. (j) The bird sang ——.

LESSON 15

ADVERBIAL PHRASES

An ADVERB stands alone as a single word. A group of words performing the same function as an adverb is called an ADVERBIAL PHRASE. **Adverbial phrases, like adverbs, answer the questions "Where?", "When?", "How?", and "How much?",** and are classified as ADVERBIAL PHRASES OF PLACE, TIME, MANNER and DEGREE.

A PHRASE is a group of words which does not make a complete statement and, unlike a CLAUSE, does not contain either subject or predicate.

Here is a table showing a few ADVERBIAL PHRASES of TIME.

ADVERBIAL PHRASES OF TIME

a short while ago	in olden times	now and again
a great many times	in a moment	once a day
again and again	in a twinkling	once a week
at once	in an instant	once a year
at present	in a flash	once in a while
at the present time	just now	once upon a time
at this time	just then	over and over again
at no time	long since	times without number
full many a time	many a time	time after time
in ancient times	now and then	week after week
in days gone by	by and by	all of a sudden

EXERCISES

1. From the above list write down any phrases which mean:
(a) a long time ago
(b) now
(c) repeatedly
(d) occasionally
(e) directly

2. Write out the ADVERBIAL PHRASES of MANNER in these sentences:
(a) The foundation stone was well and truly laid.
(b) He performed the task with a cheerful smile.
(c) The boy sat with furrowed brow.
(d) He wore a very puzzled expression.
(e) The crowd very quickly dispersed.
(f) He approached the bedside on tiptoe.
(g) He watched the film with bated breath.
(h) He opened the parcel with the utmost care.

3. In the following sentences we have some ADVERBIAL PHRASES of PLACE. Write them out and name the VERB which each qualifies, e.g.:

He ran round the corner. ADVERBIAL PHRASE—*round the corner*, qualifying the verb *ran*.

(a) The ship vanished beyond the horizon.
(b) The wreckage was scattered far and wide.
(c) He fell by the wayside.
(d) The scouts camped beside the stream.
(e) The refugees came from distant lands.
(f) The path wound through the woods.
(g) The daffodils grew beneath the trees.
(h) The sound of the firing echoed across the valley.
(i) He was pushed from pillar to post.
(j) The aircraft flew over the hill.

ADVERBS of DEGREE or QUANTITY are usually expressed in ONE WORD such as, most, fully, nearly, firstly (or first), quite, too, almost, secondly, enough.

4. Use each of those words once only in the following sentences:

(a) You must —— learn to obey and —— to speak the truth.
(b) Have you had —— to eat?
(c) He was —— unhappy.
(d) He had —— much to eat.
(e) I —— succeeded.
(f) He was —— run over.
(g) He was not —— conscious.
(h) I am —— well thank you.

5. Write out the ADVERBIAL PHRASES from the following sentences and state to which class each belongs, e.g.:

I saw you last night. ADVERBIAL PHRASE OF TIME—*last night.*

(a) He dashed round the corner.
(b) "Three fishers went sailing away to the West."
(c) We visited France a long time ago.

(d) The sun sets behind the hills.

(e) Bats and swallows drink while on the wing.

(f) I will come as soon as I can.

(g) The car was driven without due care.

(h) Rooks return from foraging just before dark.

(i) I go to the cinema very often.

(j) I will bring the book tomorrow morning.

(k) Every now and then she gave a shout of joy.

(l) The girl read the passage with feeling and understanding.

(6) Here are some ADVERBS of TIME, MANNER, PLACE, and DEGREE.

They are all mixed up. Draw four short columns and place each adverb in the right column:

never, ever, bravely, more, weekly, almost, rapidly, above, there, here, sufficiently, much.

7. Here are three ADVERBS of PLACE—DOWN, UNDER, ACROSS. Draw three columns, each having one of these words at the top. Place the following NOUNS and VERBS in the right columns:

girder, sink, subject (verb), dive, transept, subway, trans-Atlantic, subterranean, drop, hurtle, trans-Siberian, submit, swoop, tumble, avalanche, submarine, transact, transmit.

LESSON 16

PREPOSITIONS (1)

A PREPOSITION is a word which is placed **before a NOUN or PRONOUN to show its relation to some other word mentioned in the sentence**, e.g.:

(1) The ship sailed *under* the bridge.

"Under" is a PREPOSITION because it shows the connection between "ship" and "bridge".

(2) The river flows *through* the town.

"Through" is a PREPOSITION because it shows the connection between "river" and "town".

Some of the PREPOSITIONS used most often are:

about, above, after, against, along, amid, amidst, among, amongst, around, at, before, behind, below, beneath, beside, between, betwixt, beyond, by, down, during, except, for, from, in, into, near, of, off, on, over, round, since, through, till, to, towards, under, underneath, until, unto, up, upon, with, within, without.

PREPOSITIONS often express **position, cause,** or **direction.** A preposition is said to GOVERN the NOUN or PRONOUN which follows it.

Most prepositions may also be used as ADVERBS, but the two uses must be carefully distinguished. A PREPOSITION is *always* followed by a NOUN or PRONOUN.

PREPOSITIONS	ADVERBS
He walked *by* the window.	He walked *by.*
I looked *up* the hill.	I looked *up.*
He remained *behind* the door.	He remained *behind.*

EXERCISES

1. Name the PREPOSITIONS in the following sentences and state the NOUN or PRONOUN which each governs.

(a) He found the pheasant's egg among the bracken.
(b) There were bright intervals between the showers.
(c) Daffodils grew beneath the trees.
(d) Away she went from her accustomed place.
(e) She sent him off the premises.
(f) He was left without a penny.
(g) He could not agree with me on this occasion.
(h) The dog leaped over the wall into the garden.

2. Which of these PREPOSITIONS would you put in the sentences that follow?

upon, before, between, without, from, on, across, at, beside, beneath.

(a) The prisoner stood —— the judge.
(b) She left me —— a murmur.
(c) They had come far —— their homes.
(d) He fell —— the rails.
(e) Your blood be —— your own head.
(f) The river glided —— the bridge.
(g) I hope I can rely —— you.
(h) You will be awakened —— dawn.
(i) He found the ball —— the bat.
(j) He sailed —— the ocean.

3. Now supply the correct prepositions in these spaces:
(a) He is very good —— arithmetic.
(b) The medicine is very good —— coughs.
(c) The book is interesting only —— parts.
(d) Will you supply me —— four cakes?
(e) Write —— the editor —— a free copy —— this book.
(f) I do not agree —— Sam.

We have seen that a PHRASE is a group of words which makes sense but not complete sense. Many phrases begin with a PREPOSITION.

4. Point out the phrases which begin with a PREPOSITION in the following sentences:
(a) He fell underneath the bus.
(b) He was far from home.
(c) He was near death.
(d) The aeroplane flew across the desert.
(e) For some time he lay betwixt life and death.
(f) He recovered after many weeks.

64

Special Prepositions

Among and *amongst*

These must be used when speaking of more than two persons or things, e.g.:

He fell *among* thieves. The clothes were distributed *amongst* the poor.

Beside and *besides*

Beside means *near* or *next to*, e.g.:

He sat *beside* me.

Besides means *as well as* or *in addition*, e.g.:

There are other prepositions *besides* those I have mentioned.

In means "staying or remaining in one place", e.g.:

The bird was *in* its nest.

Into shows movement, e.g., The boy fell *into* the pond.
Between should be used only when speaking of TWO persons or things.
At is used with the names of **small** towns and villages, e.g.:

He was residing *at* Banbury.

In is also used with names of **larger** towns and countries, e.g.:

He is staying *in* Germany.

By is generally followed by the name of a person or thing doing something, e.g.:

This play was written *by* Shakespeare.

With is generally followed by the implement used, e.g.:

He struck him *with* a knife.

Double Prepositions

These consist of **two** PREPOSITIONS forming **one** expression, e.g.:
far off, from out, from behind, from beneath, from over, out of, in between, etc.

65

5. From the words in brackets choose the correct PREPOSITION to complete the following sentences:

(a) The cat was chased —— a dog. (by, with)
(b) He shared the sweets —— the two boys. (among, between)
(c) The spider sat down —— Miss Muffet. (besides, beside)
(d) My sister was born —— Manchester. (in, at)
(e) The prisoner was found innocent —— the crime. (for, of, from)
(f) The motorist swerved —— a lamp standard. (in, into)
(g) He lived —— human habitation. (far off, far from)
(h) The boys divided the cake —— themselves. (amongst, between)

LESSON 17

PREPOSITIONS (2)

Certain PREPOSITIONS must follow particular verbs or adjectives. It may be any part of the verb or adjective.

Here is a list of PREPOSITIONS which should follow these VERBS:

To absolve from
To adapt for (a purpose)
To afflict with
To agree to (a proposal)
To agree with (someone)
To agree upon (a plan)
To aim at
To be angry with
To be ashamed of (somebody)
To arrive at (a house, village, town, another place, decision)
To arrive in (a city, country, other very important place)
To attend to (to listen)
To attend upon (to wait upon)
To blame for
To change for (something)
To change with (somebody)
To comment on
To compare to (a thing)
To compare with (a person or thing)

To complain of

To confide in (to place confidence in)

To confide to (to entrust to)

To consist of

To correspond to (a thing)

To correspond with (a person)

To contrast with (a person or thing)

To descend from

To despair of

To die of

To differ with (somebody)

To differ from (opinion)

To divide among (many)

To divide between (two)

To disagree with

To disapprove of

To discourage from

To profit by

To part with (something)

To part from (somebody)

To prevail upon

To protest against

To rely on

To suffer from

To wait for (person, thing)

To wait upon (somebody)

To write to (somebody)

To write about (something)

EXERCISES

1. Complete these sentences with the appropriate PREPOSITIONS which follow the VERBS:

(a) The boy was told to write —— his favourite sport.

(b) The councillors had to wait —— the mayor.

(c) She died —— a broken heart.

(d) He said that he would discourage me —— any further adventures.

(e) The doctor despaired —— his life.

(f) The class was asked to compare one specimen —— another.

(g) He was going to confer —— me —— the matter.

(h) He was afflicted —— total blindness.

(i) He arrived —— a definite conclusion.

(j) He arrived —— London feeling very tired.

2. Make the second sentence in each pair mean the same as the first by filling in the missing words, one of which must be a PREPOSITION:

(a) He was totally blind.
    He was afflicted ....

(b) The book will cost at least fifty pence.
You cannot buy the book ....

(c) Your behaviour shames me.
I am ashamed ....

(d) The lesson will need your attention.
You must attend ....

(e) We think alike.
I agree ....

(f) He died broken-hearted.
He died ....

(g) He wrote to his friend in Australia.
He corresponded ....

In the same way, certain PREPOSITIONS must follow particular ADJECTIVES. Here are some of them:

according to	grateful for (a kindness)
accompanied by	grateful to (a person)
accustomed to	indignant at (something)
conscious of	indignant with (somebody)
different from	ignorant of
disgusted at (something)	innocent of
disgusted with (somebody)	similar to
equal to	worthy of
full of	tired of (something)
filled with	tired with (action)
good for	vexed at (something)
guilty of	vexed with (somebody)

3. Complete these sentences with the appropriate PREPOSITIONS which follow the ADJECTIVES:

(a) He read a passage from the Gospel according —— St. John.

(b) I am fully conscious —— the wrong I have done you.

(c) I am disgusted —— your behaviour.

(d) He was equal —— anything.

(e) I am grateful —— you —— your kindness.

(f) He is full —— his own importance.

(g) He was absolutely good —— nothing.

(h) The judge found him guilty —— manslaughter.
(i) Your action is worthy —— the highest praise.
(j) I am utterly tired —— your continual chattering.
(k) He was very vexed —— me.
(l) He was very vexed —— my behaviour.

LESSON 18

CONJUNCTIONS AND INTERJECTIONS

A CONJUNCTION is really a word that **joins together other words or groups of words.** Some of the CONJUNCTIONS most frequently used are:

and, but, so, either, neither, nor, although, before, if, after, that, unless, when, while, until, since, etc.

The word CONJUNCTION comes from a Latin word which means "join together" and this is what conjunctions do. They may join together:

(a) NOUNS, such as Jack *and* Jill went up the hill.
     This is much simpler than saying,
                    Jack went up the hill.
                    Jill went up the hill.
     In the same way they may join together:
(b) ADJECTIVES—
     e.g.: The sky was bright *and* cloudless.
(c) VERBS—
     e.g.: Grin *and* bear it.
(d) ADVERBS—
     e.g.: Steadily *and* gradually we gained on him.
(e) PHRASES—
     e.g.: He was in great pain *but* out of danger.
(f) SENTENCES—
     e.g.: He could write well, *but* he could not do arithmetic.
           I was afraid *lest* he should fall.
           I did not say anything *because* she was frightened.

69

Sometimes small phrases in themselves are CONJUNCTIONS, e.g., *so that, as soon as*:

I walked quickly *so that* I could catch him *as soon as* he came out of his office.

Some words can be other parts of speech as well as conjunctions:

He left the room *after* I had spoken.

(CONJUNCTION)

Jill came tumbling *after*.

(ADVERB)

The man ran *after* the bus.

(PREPOSITION)

EXERCISES

1. State the two sentences implied or expressed in each of the following examples and the CONJUNCTION which joins them:
(a) Mary is a stupid and idle girl.
(b) Neither your friend nor mine will be present.
(c) Either you will go or I will.
(d) You will come when you are called.
(e) He felt faint whilst they were singing the hymn.

2. Pick out the CONJUNCTIONS in the following sentences:
(a) He went for a walk although it was raining.
(b) I am unable to work while you are making such a noise.
(c) I shall not go unless you come too.
(d) He did not know where he was going.
(e) You must remain at the hotel tonight since it is too late to go on.
(f) You must continue your journey before the sun sets.
(g) He was afraid lest I should be late.
(h) He was ill so he remained at home.

3. Using a conjunction, combine the following groups of words each into ONE SENTENCE:

(a) Shakespeare wrote "The Merchant of Venice".
    He is regarded as one of the world's greatest poets.
(b) He went for a walk.
    He returned home. It was raining.
(c) My mother went shopping.
    She forgot her basket.
    She went back.
(d) I was going for a walk.
    I met a fox.
    The fox ran into the woods.
(e) The boy was lonely.
    He met his friend.
(f) I shall stay.
    You tell me to go.

Interjections

Some people consider that the INTERJECTION is not a part of speech. It is really an expression of EMOTION, such as, *Oh! Ha! Hullo! Stop!*

An INTERJECTION should always be followed by the EX-CLAMATION MARK (!).

Sometimes an interjection is an abbreviated form of a whole sentence, as:

Alas! or *Alack!* which means "I am sorry".
Farewell! which means "May you fare well!"
Goodbye! which means "God be with you!"

INTERJECTIONS often express feelings of approval, attention, concern, contempt, joy, reflection, relief, surprise, annoyance, etc.

4. In these sentences pick out the words which are INTER-JECTIONS and say what feeling or state of mind you think each expresses:

(a) Good gracious! I shall miss my train.

71

(b) Hurrah! I have passed my examination.

(c) Hullo! I did not expect to see you here.

(d) Bravo! You have done well.

(e) Oh dear! what a calamity! She is badly hurt.

(f) Hm! I shall have to consider this matter.

(g) Bother! I have mislaid my pen.

(h) At last! that's finished.

(i) Hush! You will wake the baby.

(j) Hark! I hear the sound of Christmas bells.

LESSON 19

COMMON MISTAKES (1)

Nouns, Pronouns

There are a great many everyday errors that people frequently make. Some of them have already been mentioned, but a careful study of this grammar book should enable us to detect other mistakes.

Sensible people learn from their errors, and we should always carefully examine all written work which has been returned to us, and note all the mistakes which have been pointed out. It is a good plan to write out these mistakes as corrections, and not to make them again.

Many of us may find difficulty with spelling, but we can overcome this if we make a habit of looking up words in a dictionary and if we actually learn words which give us trouble, such as *occasion, necessary, receive, beginning,* etc.

Mistakes in grammar are not so easy to detect, but they should be corrected, as well as spelling mistakes.

Here are a few mistakes often made with NOUNS and PRO-NOUNS:

1. PROPER NOUNS without CAPITAL LETTERS.

All PROPER NOUNS must be written with a CAPITAL LETTER, e.g.: the days of the week, the months of the year, continents, oceans, rivers, lakes, mountains, and the names of towns, cities, and persons. Titles of books should always start with capital letters, and so should the first word of a sentence after a full stop, e.g.:

We are going home on *Saturday*.
March is a windy month.
Greece is sometimes called the "Birthplace of Democracy".
London stands on the river *Thames*.
Lake Superior is one of the five *Great Lakes*.
Mount Everest is the highest mountain in the world.
Charles Dickens wrote *"Oliver Twist"*.

However, we must also remember that in English COMMON NOUNS do **not** need a CAPITAL LETTER and it is wrong to put them in unnecessarily.

EXERCISES

1. Place CAPITAL LETTERS where necessary in the following sentences:
(a) i am going to manchester on tuesday.
(b) shakespeare was a famous english poet who was born at stratford-on-avon. he wrote many plays including henry V.
(c) i went for a walk along high street.
(d) the boy read the lesson from the gospel according to st. luke.
(e) mary and joan both live in oak terrace.

WRONG SINGULARS and PLURALS
When the NOUN refers to ONE object it is said to be SINGULAR; when it refers to MORE THAN ONE object it is said to be PLURAL.

73

If I say "Mathematics are very difficult to learn", the sentence is wrong. *Mathematics* is the name of one subject and therefore we should say, "Mathematics *is* very difficult to learn."

"We ourself were left behind." This should be:

"We *ourselves* were left behind."

"The trees were covered with leafs." The plural of *leaf* is *leaves*; hence we should say: "The trees were covered with leaves."

"I saw four sheeps on the hill." Both the singular and plural form is *sheep*.

Many mistakes are made with—

EACH, EVERY and NEITHER.

These are all SINGULAR and must be followed by a verb in the singular, e.g.:

Each of them *was* running towards the gate. (NOT *were*)

Neither of the boys *is* here. (NOT *are*)

Every one of the pens *was* lost. (NOT *were*)

Many people say "There *was* some boys playing."

Boys is plural and requires a verb in the plural form.

Say: "There *were* some boys playing."

EXERCISES

2. Write the following sentences correctly:

(a) The boys did this theirselfs.

(b) The jars was on the shelfs.

(c) The cows is being milked and together they give two pails full.

(d) We have two Harries and two Jennies in the class.

(e) Each of them were present.

(f) Every one of the girls were absent.

(g) Neither John nor Jim were able to come.

THE PRONOUN.

Many mistakes are made in the use of PRONOUNS, especially the RELATIVE PRONOUNS *who, whom, whose, which, that.*

The correct use of these pronouns has already been shown on page 27.

PERSONAL PRONOUNS IN WRONG ORDER
It is considered impolite or uncivil to say:
"I and my friend" or "I and Mary". It is better to say "My friend and I" or "Mary and I".

PREPOSITIONS AT THE END OF QUESTIONS
In modern English it is acceptable to say either:
From whom did you get this?
For what do you want it? *or*
Who did you get this from?
What do you want it for?

In fact, the second form of such questions—with the preposition at the end—is more used today; and to say "For what do you want it?' now sounds pedantic.
Whom is used less today than formerly, and it is usually acceptable to say either:
Whom did you get this from? *or*
Who did you get this from?

ANTECEDENTS AND RELATIVE PRONOUNS
The noun or pronoun which goes before a RELATIVE PRONOUN and to which the relative pronoun refers is call the ANTECEDENT. *Book* is the antecedent of *which* in this sentence:
Here is the book which I promised you.

As far as possible, it is best to have the ANTECEDENT and the RELATIVE PRONOUN together. For example, this is not a good sentence:
I drove in a small car across the mountain which had only three wheels.
It would be better as:
I drove across the mountain in a small car which had only three wheels.

Sometimes the relative pronoun does not relate to the noun immediately in front of it, but to the idea or fact in the preceding group of words, e.g.:

Joe ran noisily into the classroom, which annoyed the teacher.

EXERCISES

3. Point out any mistakes in these sentences, and rewrite the the sentences correctly:

(a) This is the dog what stole the meat.
(b) I and William chased the thief.
(c) The boy took the bicycle to the shed which needed a new tyre.
(d) The two girls gave the child a piece of chocolate whose leg had been hurt in the accident.

LESSON 20

COMMON MISTAKES (2)

Adjectives and Adverbs

ADJECTIVES
Wrong use of DEGREES OF COMPARISON
Adjectives have three degrees of comparison.

1. This is the best of the two books.
   In that sentence *best* is wrong, because *best* is the SUPER-LATIVE DEGREE (good, better, best), and can only be used when comparing three or more. The sentence should be:
   This is the *better* of the two books.

2. He is more taller than his mother.

   In that sentence *more* is wrong, because *taller* means *more tall*, and we do not need the word *more*. The sentence should be:

   He is taller than his mother.

3. It was the most silliest joke.

   In that sentence *most* is wrong, because *silliest* means *most silly*, and we do not need the word *most*. The sentence should be:

   It was the silliest joke.

   We must also remember that certain adjectives are superlative in themselves, e.g.:

perfect, square, extreme, etc.

   We cannot have anything "more square" than "square".

USING A PRONOUN INSTEAD OF AN ADJECTIVE.

   People often make statements like this:

   I do not like *them* cakes.

   Them is a PRONOUN in the "objective" case. We should use a "pointing out" or "demonstrative" ADJECTIVE instead.

   We should say:

   I do not like *those* cakes.

LACK OF AGREEMENT BETWEEN ADJECTIVE AND NOUN.

(1) Where did you find *those kind* of pencils?

(2) Where did you buy *these sort* of tomatoes?

   An ADJECTIVE must agree in number with the NOUN it describes. *Kind* and *sort* are SINGULAR NOUNS; *those* and *these* are PLURAL ADJECTIVES which should be changed to the SINGULAR.

   We should say:

(1) Where did you find *that kind* of pencil?

(2) Where did you buy *this sort* of tomato?

If there is more than one kind or sort, the PLURAL of BOTH noun and adjective must be used, e.g.:

(1) Where did you find *those kinds* of pencils?
(2) Where did you buy *these sorts* of tomatoes?

WRONG USE OF "EITHER" AND "ANY"
Examine these sentences:

(1) You may choose *either* of the *four* presents.
(2) You may have *any* of the *two* books for your birthday.

Either means a choice between *two* alternatives.
(*Note:* the word *alternative* is often misused, It means "one or other of *two things only.*" Thus *three alternatives* is wrong. You should say "a choice of three things.")
Any means a choice between *more* than *two.*
Hence we should say:

(1) You may choose *any* of the *four* presents.
(2) You may have *either* of the *two* books for your birthday.

The "FIRST TWO" and the "TWO FIRST"
I read only the two first chapters of the book.
There cannot be two first chapters of a book. We should say:
I read only the first two chapters of the book.

EXERCISES

1. Point out any mistakes in these sentences, and rewrite the sentences correctly:

(a) She was the shortest of the two sisters.
(b) Where are you going on the three first days of your holiday?
(c) This is the most funniest story of all.
(d) The first film was more duller than the second.
(e) Select either of the ten pictures and put them there.
(f) You may choose any of the two hats.

Adverbs

Speak as loud as you can.
She sang very beautiful.
Loud and *beautiful* are adjectives and cannot qualify verbs. We should say:
Speak as *loudly* as you can.
She sang very *beautifully*.

In certain sentences with such verbs as: *appear, feel, look, smell, sound, taste* we must be careful with adjectives and adverbs.
The boy looked weak.
The boy looked weakly at his father.
In the first of those sentences we are considering the appearance of the boy himself. In the second sentence we are considering the way the boy's eyes gazed at the father.
Notice these sentences also:
This cloth feels rough.
She felt the cloth roughly and threw it aside.

DOUBLE NEGATIVES
I am not doing nothing about it.
He would never go there no more.

Those sentences are wrong and should be:

I am *not* doing *anything* about it.
He would *not* go there *any* more.

Similarly, this sentence is wrong:

For three weeks he never spoke to nobody.

It should be:

For three weeks he *never* spoke to *anybody*.

ADJECTIVES AND ADVERBS WITH *LY*
Some adjectives end with *ly*, e.g.: *friendly, silly, cowardly, lively*.
Adverbs are not formed from such adjectives by adding *ly* as is usual with most other adjectives, e.g.: *sweet* (adjective)—*sweetly*

79

(adverb). We do not say *friendlyly*. Nor can those adjectives be used as adverbs even though they end with "*ly*" like most adverbs. If we want to use *friendly* to qualify a verb, we say *in a friendly manner* or *in a friendly way*. Similarly, this sentence is wrong:

The actress sang lovely.

It should be:

The actress sang with a lovely voice.

EXERCISES

2. Write out these sentences correctly:

(a) Come home as quick as you can.
(b) This soup tastes nicely.
(c) He never lent me nothing.
(d) Nobody went nowhere yesterday.
(e) Write as clear as you can.
(f) That story sounds strangely.
(g) The car appeared sudden round the corner.
(h) He shouted at me unfriendly.

LESSON 21

REVISION TEST (2)

A. 1. State which PREPOSITIONS are used after the following:

(a) guilty ——
(b) deficient ——
(c) impatient ——
(d) accompanied ——
(e) insist ——
(f) comply ——
(g) familiar ——
(h) free ——
(i) different ——
(j) provide ——

2. Fill in the blank spaces with the correct form of the ADJEC-
TIVE on the LEFT and state whether it is in the POSITIVE,
COMPARATIVE, or SUPERLATIVE DEGREE.

(a) HEALTHY   John was the —— of the two boys.
(b) SHORT   He was the —— boy in the class.
(c) EXCITING   This story is —— than that.
(d) LATE   Of all those who did not arrive punctually,
                 he was the ——.
(e) BAD   He was the —— boy in the school.
(f) DISAGREEABLE His task was the —— of all.
(g) LITTLE   He has —— patience than I have.
(h) PLEASANT   She was the —— of the two girls.

3. Give a name to something that:
(a) measures heat.
(b) shows the direction of the wind.
(c) makes objects from a distance appear nearer.
(d) makes small objects appear larger.
(e) causes objects to fall to the ground.
(f) is a kind of moving staircase.
(g) measures the pressure of the air.
(h) is an instrument which helps one to determine direction.
(i) sometimes swings from a clock.
(j) is an instrument which measures electric current.

4. With what number do you associate the following?
(a) quadrilateral   (e) centurion   (h) pentagon
(b) hexagon   (f) score   (i) monologue
(c) decade   (g) gross   (j) tripod
(d) triangle

B. 1. On the left-hand side are some NOUNS. On the right are
      some sentences. Write out these sentences with the correct
      ADJECTIVES formed from these NOUNS.

(a) FIRE   He had a very —— temper.
(b) CHILD   He acted in a —— manner.

(c) PITY   He was in a most —— plight.
(d) MERCY   He was a very —— king.
(e) BODY   He suffered no —— injury.
(f) COURAGE Marlborough was a clever and —— soldier.
(g) RESOURCE Clive was a very —— general.
(h) SIMPLICITY She cannot do the —— sum.

2. Write these sentences in the PLURAL form:

(a) This shelf has on it a plate, cup, and saucer.
(b) This baby has one tooth.
(c) The roof of this house needs to be repaired as it is not water-tight.
(d) I caught a salmon in the river.
(e) In the zoo he saw a monkey, a deer, a donkey and an antelope.

3. What do we call a person who

(a) Tests people's eyes?
(b) Cares for teeth?
(c) Cuts hair?
(d) Mends shoes?
(e) Operates upon people?
(f) Presides at a trial?
(g) Gives the verdicts at a trial?
(h) Carves out of stone?
(i) Attends to sick animals?
(j) Sells hats for ladies?
(k) Collects stamps?

4. In the following sentences state whether the word in italics is a PRONOUN or an ADJECTIVE:

(a) *Those* are delicious cakes.
(d) *Those* cakes are delicious.
(c) *His* satchel hangs on *that* peg.
(d) *Those* shoes are *his*.
(e) *Each* child was given an orange.
(f) *Each* was questioned in turn.
(g) *What* was the correct time?
(h) *What* time is it?

C. 1. Draw four columns headed ADVERBS of MANNER, TIME, PLACE, and DEGREE, and place the following ADVERBS in the correct column:

quickly	yesterday	tomorrow	above
weekly	below	anxiously	bravely
far	scarcely	immediately	very
nearly	anywhere	courageously	beyond
easily	few	since	almost

2. What PART OF SPEECH is each of the words in italics?

(a) Do you *like* toffee?

(b) I shall not see his *like* again.

(c) With *like* words she persuaded him.

(d) He slept *like* a top.

(e) He did not know *that*.

(f) *That* boy is late.

(g) Did he say *that* he could come?

(h) It is a *warm* day.

(i) Do you feel *warm*?

(j) Mother will *warm* the milk for baby.

3. Rewrite these sentences in the FUTURE TENSE:

(a) I am walking across the fields today.

(b) He is trying hard with his work this term.

(c) It is my birthday today.

(d) The girls play hockey today.

(e) The flowers are very beautiful this spring.

4. Give the PERSON and NUMBER of each verb in these sentences:

(a) *I am going* on my holidays tomorrow.

(b) *They were applauding* continuously.

(c) When *are you coming* home, Mary?

(d) *Will you* please *go away*, boys?

(e) The boys *ran away*.

(f) *We play* in the park after school.

PUNCTUATION

In order to make our meaning clear when we write English we must punctuate properly. Punctuation shows how words should be grouped, and the placing of a comma may make all the difference.

There is the well-known sentence about King Charles's head:

Charles the First walked and talked half an hour after his head was cut off.

This is nonsense as it stands, but, if properly punctuated, makes sense:

Charles the First walked and talked; half an hour after, his head was cut off.

Here is another sentence:

The judge said the prisoner is unfair.

If punctuated thus:

"The judge," said the prisoner, "is unfair", it has an entirely different meaning from:

The judge said, "The prisoner is unfair."

The chief PUNCTUATION MARKS are:

1. The full stop .
2. The comma ,
3. The question mark ?
4. The exclamation mark !
5. The semicolon ;
6. The colon :
7. The apostrophe '
8. The dash —
9. The hyphen -
10. Quotation marks " " *or* ' ' *or* " ' ' "

A sentence should normally **begin with a capital letter** and should **end with a full stop.**

A comma is used **to denote a shorter pause,** or **to mark off a series of words or groups of words,** e.g.:
In the shopping basket there were potatoes, oranges, bananas, and lemons.

The question mark is used **after a question,** e.g.:
Are you going home tonight?

The exclamation mark is used to **express sudden emotion or surprise,** e.g.:
Alas! I have lost my way.

Both the semicolon and colon are used to **denote a longer pause than a comma.**

The apostrophe **shows that one or more letters have been left out,** e.g.: was not = wasn't. You will = you'll. It is = it's, etc.
It is also used to show possession.
This boy's cap (of one boy)
These boys' caps (of several boys)
In the case of a PLURAL noun, such as "The women's entrance", the apostrophe comes before the "s".

The dash is used to show that there is **a break in what a person is saying,** e.g.:
I— er— do not know.

It is sometimes used when a person's name is written with the initial letter only, e.g.: A certain Mr. B— was seen last night.

The hyphen is **shorter than the dash** and **is used to join the parts of what is known as a** COMPOUND WORD, such as, mouse-trap, milk-jug, book-keeping, etc.

Quotation marks are used:

1. To show the **actual words of a speaker,** e.g.:

   My mother said to me, "You are very untidy."

2. In **titles of books and plays,** e.g.:

   Charles Dickens wrote "Oliver Twist".

3. To **indicate quotations,** e.g.:

   "Go to the ant, thou sluggard; consider her ways, and be wise".

4. To show that a word **is used in a special sense,** e.g.:

   He met his "Waterloo".

5. To show a **quotation** WITHIN a **quotation.**

   "This," he said, "is clearly a case of 'forewarned is forearmed' ".

EXERCISES

1. Insert the necessary capital letters, full stops, commas, etc. in the following:
(a) the names of the brothers were george john richard james and brian
(b) georges brother came to tea last good friday
(c) he lives at 103 st jamess road newtown
(d) the girls mothers were walking along high street
(e) was the girls mother alone
(f) the boys entrance to the yew tree secondary modern school is in south street
(g) the unemployed man waited outside the mens entrance to the employment office

2. The following are common uses of the apostrophe. Write out in full the meaning of each:

(a) You'll   (e) Don't
(b) He's   (f) Doesn't
(c) O'er   (g) Can't
(d) Hasn't

3. These words can be used with an apostrophe. Write them with the apostrophe correctly placed:

(a) I am
(b) They are
(c) There is
(d) I did not
(e) We were not
(f) He was not
(g) You will not
(h) He should not
(i) They shall not
(j) They could not

4. Punctuate correctly and insert capital letters, etc., where necessary:

the mock turtle went on we had the best of educations in fact we went to school every day

ive been to a day school too said alice you needn't be as proud as all that

with extras asked the mock turtle a little anxiously

yes said alice we learned french and music

and washing said the mock turtle

certainly not said alice indignantly

ah then yours wasnt a really good school said the mock turtle in a tone of great relief now at ours they had at the end of the bill french music and washing extra

5. Abbreviations with initials of titles and names are written in capital letters, e.g.:

H.M. (Her Majesty).

Most abbreviations with first letters of ordinary words are written in small letters, e.g.: p.c. (per cent); but some are written in capital letters, e.g.: T.V. (television).

What do these letters mean?

B.B.C.	H.M.S.	N.B.	R.S.P.C.A.
C.I.D.	M.A.	O.H.M.S.	T.U.C.
F.A.	M.P.	P.T.O.	V.C.

Nowadays the full stops between the letters are disappearing; more and more often we see TUC, MP, etc., without full stops.

Note: "e.g.", which is often used in this book, is itself an abbreviation from Latin, *exempli gratia.* (= for example).

6. Put in punctuation marks to show that these sentences can have two meanings:

(a) The nurse says the patient is tiresome.
(b) The shopkeeper declares the boy is a thief.
(c) The manager remarks the secretary is absent.

LESSON 23

DIRECT AND INDIRECT OR REPORTED SPEECH

DIRECT SPEECH consists of the **exact words used by a speaker** and it is usually put inside inverted commas.

INDIRECT or REPORTED SPEECH gives the **remarks of the speaker** as **quoted by someone else,** and it is generally introduced by a verb of *saying* in the *past* tense. The following example should make this clear:

DIRECT SPEECH.

He observed: "I think that Robert will be here, and when he comes we will all go for a walk."

REPORTED SPEECH.

The speaker said that he thought that Robert would be there, and that when he came, they would all go for a walk.

Certain rules must be followed when turning a passage of DIRECT SPEECH into REPORTED SPEECH.

1. REPORTED SPEECH *must* be introduced by a clause containing a verb of *saying* in the *past* tense, e.g.:
He said that ——. The speaker replied that ——. The chairman observed that ——, etc.

88

2. All verbs in the *present* tense should normally be turned into verbs in the *past* tense. *Has* becomes *had*, *are* becomes *were*, *shall* becomes *should*, and *may* becomes *might*.
3. PRONOUNS of the first and second person are changed to the third. *I* becomes *he* or *she*; *we* becomes *they*; *you* becomes *he, she, they*, or *him, her, them*.
4. All words denoting *nearness* must be replaced by corresponding words of *remoteness*. Hence *now* becomes *then*, *this* becomes *that*, *my* becomes *his*, *today* becomes *that day*, *yesterday* becomes *the day before*, *hence* becomes *thence*, *ago* becomes *before*, and *thus* becomes *so*.

Here is a longer example:

DIRECT SPEECH.

"Brenda," said Jack, "will you be going down to Ilfracombe for Easter?"

"Yes," answered Brenda.

"I will take you down in my car if you like," said Jack.

"Thanks for the offer," Brenda replied, "but I am sorry I shall not be able to accept, as I already have an engagement for Good Friday."

REPORTED SPEECH.

Jack asked Brenda if she would be going down to Ilfracombe for Easter and when she replied that she would, he said that he would take her in his car if she liked. Brenda thanked him for the offer, but said she was sorry she could not accept, as she already had an engagement for Good Friday.

EXERCISES

1. Convert each of the following into REPORTED SPEECH:
(a) "Look up! look up! and guard thy head," cries the fatal voice of Haco to the king.
(b) "I believe you are all of one mind," observed the chairman.
(c) "Are the men ready, and are they prepared to work hard?"

89

(d) "Why is the plan proposed? Will it commend itself to the businessmen? Will the trade unions favour it? Who is likely to derive any benefit from such an ill-considered scheme?"

2. Here is a longer exercise taken from *Alice in Wonderland* by Lewis Carroll.

Change the following DIRECT SPEECH into REPORTED SPEECH:

"Have you guessed the riddle yet?" the Hatter said, turning to Alice again.

"No, I give it up," Alice replied: "what's the answer?"

"I haven't the slightest idea," said the Hatter.

"Nor I," said the March Hare.

Alice sighed wearily. "I think you might do something better with the time," she said, "than waste it asking riddles with no answers."

"If you knew Time as well as I do," said the Hatter, "you wouldn't talk about wasting it."

CONVERTING REPORTED SPEECH INTO DIRECT SPEECH.

Here we simply reverse the process explained above.

3. Change from REPORTED to DIRECT SPEECH the following:

(a) The doctor said that he could not give the patient permission to resume work until he had completely recovered.

(b) His mother remarked that she was sorry her son had brought home such a bad report from school. She was thoroughly ashamed of him.

(c) The policeman said that the accident was due entirely to the boy's own fault, and that he had not stopped, looked, or thought, before he stepped off the kerb.

4. Here is an exercise from *Cranford* by Mrs. Gaskell. Change the REPORTED form into DIRECT SPEECH:

Miss Matty said that her heart was sad for that little careworn child. Although the child's father was a conjurer, she looked as if she had never had a good game of play in her life. Miss Matty explained that she used to make very pretty balls in that way when she was a girl, and she thought she would try if she could not make that one smart and take it to Phoebe that afternoon. She thought, she added, that the "gang" must have left the neighbourhood, for one did not hear any more of their violence and robbery then.

Many people use the word *said* far too frequently. This is not to say it should never be used. *Said* is simply an overworked word. There are many other more expressive words which can be used instead.

To express ANGER	bawled, bellowed, chided, complained, grumbled, stormed, snapped, snarled, shouted.
ARGUMENT and DISCUSSION	admitted, affirmed, agreed, argued, confessed, declared, demanded, granted, protested, reasoned, repeated, stated, urged.
COMMAND	commanded, demanded, dictated, directed, insisted, ordered.
DISTRESS	cried, groaned, howled, lamented, moaned, sobbed.
EXCLAMATION	exclaimed.
INTERRUPTION	interrupted, interjected.
INDISTINCT SPEECH	gabbled, mumbled, muttered, stammered.
INQUIRY and REQUEST	appealed, asked, begged, demanded, entreated, inquired, pleaded.
GENERAL SPEECH	added, answered, replied, remarked, reported, observed.

5. Use these verbs in place of the words in italics in these sentences—EXCLAIM, GASP, GROAN, GROWL, ORDER, SNAP, WHINE:

(a) "Stop this noise and go away," he *said in a voice of command*.

(b) "What an extraordinary car!" he *said in a voice of wonder and surprise*.

(c) "You never give me presents," he *said in a voice of continuous complaint*.

(d) "I can't see,' he *said with a sudden catch of breath in his voice.*

(e) "I'm going to die soon," he *said in a voice of great pain.*

(f) "I'm fed up with you; never let me see you again," he *said in a low slow, angry voice.*

(g) "You ass!" he *said in a sharp rude voice.*

LESSON 24

PREFIXES AND SUFFIXES

A PREFIX is a letter or syllable added to the beginning of a word to form another word. e.g.: (word) *port*; (prefix) *im*; (new word) *import*.

A SUFFIX is a letter or syllable added to the end of a word to form another word, e.g.: (word) *eat*; (suffix) *able*; (new word) *eatable*.

EXERCISES

1. Here are five PREFIXES—*dis, im, ab, il, in*:
   Here are five words:

   normal, legal, convenient, trust, possible

   Place the right PREFIX to each of these words to give them the *opposite* meaning.

2. Here are eight words each with the PREFIX *dis*:
   disallow, discourage, discard, dispense, discord, disparage, discourse, discontent
   Which word would you use to describe an action which means:

(a) To say something which is not to a person's credit?

(b) To deal out?

(c) A talk or conversation?

92

(d) A quarrel or something which is out of tune?
(e) Not to encourage?
(f) To throw out or reject?
(g) Not to be content?
(h) Refuse to allow?

3. Add these SUFFIXES "ary", "ery", "ory" to the following:

(a) surg —
(b) compuls —
(c) bound —
(d) embroid —
(e) mission —
(f) dispens —
(g) rot —
(h) honor —
(i) diction —
(j) dilat —
(k) hist —
(l) volunt —

4. What VERBS ending in the SUFFIX *ate* may be used instead of these expressions?

(a) To place apart.
(b) To give peremptory orders.
(c) To look forward to.
(d) To copy someone or something.
(e) To disturb or distress.
(f) To increase the gravity of, to annoy.
(g) To prepare the soil.
(h) To shorten.
(i) To end.

Here is a list of twelve OLD ENGLISH PREFIXES:

PREFIX	MEANING	EXAMPLE
(a) afore, fore	in front of	foretell, forewarn
(b) after	after	afterwards
(c) be	strengthens meaning of root word or forms verbs	befall befriend
(d) by	by	by-pass
(e) forth	coming from	forthcoming
(f) mis	wrongly	misbehave, mistake

(g) out	outside	outlaw, outlive
(h) over	excess or more	overflow
(i) under	something lacking	underdone, underfed
(j) un	not	untrue
(k) with	against	withstand
(l) mid	middle	midway, mid-summer

5. Give suitable PREFIXES from the above table to the following words:

(a) — thought

(b) — pass

(c) — grown

(d) — draw

(e) — going

(f) — line

(g) — moan

(h) — growth

(i) — demeanour

(j) — usual

(k) — with

(l) — day

Many PREFIXES are derived from LATIN. Here are eighteen of them:

PREFIX	MEANING	EXAMPLE
(a) a, ab	away from	avert (to turn away from)
(b) ambi	both ways	ambiguous, ambidextrous
(c) ante	before	antediluvian
(d) bene	well	benefit, beneficial
(e) bi, bis	two or twice	bicycle, bisect, biped
(f) circum	round	circumference, circumnavigate
(g) contra	against	contradict, contraband
(h) de	down or away from	descend, depend
(i) e or ex	out of	eject, exit
(j) in	not	incapable, insecure
(k) infra	lower than	inferior, infra-red
(l) per	through	perspective, percolate
(m) post	after	postscript, postpone
(n) retro	backwards	retrograde, retrospect
(o) semi	half	semi-detached
(p) sub	under	subway, submarine
(q) trans	across	transport, transform
(r) equi	equal	equidistant

94

6. Complete the following sentences using a word with a suitable PREFIX from the above list:

(a) The enemy —— torpedoed the merchant ship.
(b) The magician —— him into a butterfly.
(c) We live in a —— house.
(d) The sea air — was to the invalid's health.
(e) A two-legged animal is called a ——.
(f) The climber slipped because he had an —— foothold.
(g) The smugglers hid the —— in the cave.
(h) A corporal is —— in rank to a sergeant.
(i) He could write equally well with either hand, so he could be described as ——.
(j) Drake was the first Englishman to —— the globe.

Here are a few of the better-known Greek PREFIXES:

PREFIX	MEANING	EXAMPLE
(a) an *or* ana	without	anarchy (without order)
(b) amphi	on both sides *or* all about	amphibious amphitheatre
(c) anti	against	anti-aircraft
(d) auto	self	automatic
(e) dia	through	diagonal
(f) hemi	half	hemisphere
(g) mono *or* mon	single *or* alone	monoplane
(h) penta	five	pentagon
(i) peri	around	perimeter
(j) poly	many	polygon (many sided)
(k) pro	before	prologue (speech said before)
(l) syn	with	synonym
(m) tele	from *or* afar	telegram

95

7. Give a word containing one of the above PREFIXES which has the following meaning:

(a) The behaviour of a person who acts against society.
(b) (Writing) The story of one's own life.
(c) The transmission of pictures from a long distance.
(d) A word of identical meaning with another.
(e) A school or institution where many subjects are taught.
(f) A single eyeglass.
(g) Lack of blood.
(h) A straight line passing through the centre of any body or geometrical figure.

LESSON 25

SOME SPELLING RULES

Many people find difficulty with spelling. Here are some points to bear in mind:

1. One way to learn to spell correctly is to learn regularly about ten words each day from a spelling book where words with similar endings are usually grouped together.

2. Another way is to jot down in our notebooks any words with which we find difficulty and learn them.

3. We should always write out and correct any spelling mistakes we have made in our written work.

4. We should constantly consult a dictionary, where words are given in alphabetical order, with their spelling, their meanings, pronunciation, and often derivation.

Here are a few spelling rules:

(a) Words of one syllable ending with a single vowel and a single consonant (except W and X) double the consonant before another syllable or ED, e.g.: *beg: beggar; knit: knitting; drum: drummer; rub: rubbed; fun: funny.*

96

(b) Words of more than one syllable ending with a single vowel and a single consonant (except L, W, X) and with the accent or stress on the final syllable double the consonant before another syllable or ED, e.g.: *forbid: forbidden; occur: occurred; begin: beginner, beginning.* But note *suffer: suffered* and *offer: offered.*

(c) W and X are never doubled, e.g.: *box: boxer; screw: screwed.*

(d) Words ending with EL double the L before ED and also before another syllable except on the few occasions when that syllable begins with a consonant, e.g.: *traveller; quarrelled; compelling; libellous; cancellation,* but *quarrelsome, unparalleled.*

(e) No simple and useful rule can be made for words ending with AL, IL, OL, UL, e.g.: *devilish; councillor; appalling; finalise; controlled; petroleum.*

(f) Generally a word ending with LL loses one L when it is part of another word, e.g.: *wonderful; almost; skilful; fulfil,* but there are some exceptions, e.g.: *fullness; refill.*

(g) *All right* should be written in two words and not *alright.*

(h) When EI or IE has the sound of EE (as in the word *feel*), the I comes before the E except after C, e.g.: *grief, piece; ceiling; receive.* Note, however, *seize.*

(i) Verbs ending with E generally lose the E before ING, e.g.: *come: coming; hope: hoping.* Note, however, *singe: singeing; age: ageing; dye: dyeing.* Similarly the E disappears before ABLE, e.g.: *movable, unmistakable, unshakable, but the* E is kept after C and G, e.g.: *manageable, noticeable.*

(j) Plural of words ending with Y. If the letter before Y is a vowel, add S, e.g.: *valleys; chimneys; days; toys.* If the letter before Y is a consonant, change the Y to I and add ES, e.g.: *penny: pennies; cry: cries; baby: babies.*

EXERCISES

Here are some words commonly misspelt:

accommodate	difference	immediately	prejudice
acquire	dilapidate	incite	privilege
appear	disappear	independent	really
believe	disappoint	itinerary	receive
business	dissolve	laboratory	recommend
category	eligible	legible	seize
committee	embarrass	miscellaneous	separate
comparative	exaggerate	mischievous	similarly
conscientious	glamorous	mortgage	specimen
conscious	grammar	necessary	straight
consensus	harass	occasion	supersede
criticize	humour	occurred	until
despair	humorous	omitted	usually
development	imaginary	persuade	weird

EXERCISES

1. Write out these sentences in full, inserting the correct letter or letters in the space provided:

(a) I felt scar—d when I saw the old sailor's war-scar—d face and crippled limbs.

(b) They offer—d her the roses, but she prefer—d the carnations.

(c) The jewel—r showed the lad—s and gentlemen some marvel—s brooches.

(d) "I have rec—ved cards from all my nephews and n—ces," said my aunt proudly.

(e) "I was begin—g to bel—ve you were not com—g after all."

(f) The postman made several journ—s to deliver all the repl—s to the invitation.

Words which often present special difficulty

Note HEIGHT and WEIGHT and EIGHTH, e.g.:

The height was one-eighth of a metre.

Note TO and TOO and TWO

To is a preposition, e.g.:

I am going *to* the grocer's shop *to* buy some tea.

Too is an adverb meaning *too much.*

This car is *too* small for the whole family.

Too has the additional meaning of also, e.g.:

The potatoes are bad, and the beans, *too.*

Two expresses a number e.g.:

Our team won by *two* goals to nil.

Note THERE and THEIR.

Their shows possession or belonging, e.g.:

This is *their* house. We are *their* friends. This is *their* mother.

It is a pointing-out adjective, or it may be a PRONOUN if we say:

It was *theirs*. (belonging to them)

THERE denotes a place and is also used to introduce a part of the verb *to be*, e.g.:

He is sitting over there. (adverb of place)

There will be some rain this evening.

AS and HAS

AS is a conjunction: I cannot see *as* I have no glasses.

I cannot walk *as* I am badly injured.

HAS is a verb: He *has* a cold.

She *has* measles.

IS and HIS

IS: He *is* not here. (verb)

She *is* not present. (verb)

HIS shows it belongs to him.

This is *his* cap. (pointing out adjective)

This is *his* (pronoun).

WHERE and WERE

WHERE refers to a place, e.g.: I do not know *where* to go. (adverb of place)

WERE is part of a verb, e.g: They *were* lost.

What *were* you doing?

WEAR and WARE

WEAR is a verb, e.g.:

I shall *wear* my jacket. (verb)

WARE is a noun mostly used in the plural, e.g:

The pedlar displayed his *wares*.

I like this glassware.

OFF and OF

The sound tells which preposition should be used, e.g.:

He bought a pound *of* apples.

She got *off* the bus.

BEEN and BEING

He had *been* fishing. (past tense)

You are *being* a nuisance. (present tense)

EXERCISE

2. Write out the following with the correct word from the brackets:

(a) He had (to, too, two) far to go in the time.

(b) They (were, where) going fishing.

(c) I must (ware, were, wear) my best clothes.

(d) (Their, there) house is on fire.

(e) She is standing over (their, there) in the corner.

(f) It is (alright, all right, allright) for you to stay.

(g) It is not (write, wright, right, rite) that you should do this.

(h) She had some sweet smelling (sent, scent, cent).

(i) This is (is, his) coat.

(j) He (his, is) not coming today.

(k) She (as, has) a cold.

(l) (As, has) I was walking along the High Street I saw the boy fall (of, off) his bicycle.

(m) Girls (all ways, always) talk (too, to, two) much.

100

SOME WORDS OFTEN CONFUSED

(Examples are sometimes given to illustrate meaning)

WORD	MEANING	WORD	MEANING
air	the atmosphere	alley	narrow passage
heir	one who succeeds	ally (noun)	friend
ere	before	(verb)	to combine
e'er	ever		
accede	to agree	allowed	permitted
exceed	do more	aloud	loudly, audibly
accept	to receive	altar	a holy table
except	excluding	alter	to change
addition	something added	ant	an insect
edition	literary work	aunt	a female relation
adds	vb. add	arc	part of a curve
adze	axe	ark	kind of boat
advice (noun)	help	ascent	upward move-ment
to advise (verb)	to give help	assent	to agree (verb) agreement (noun)
affect (verb)	to cause a change	ate	(past tense of verb to eat)
effect (verb) (noun)	bring about result	eight	number
ail	to be ill	aught, ought	anything
ale	a drink	ought	must or should
all	everyone		
awl	shoemaker's tool		

WORD	MEANING	WORD	MEANING
bad	not good	bell	a metal cup
bade	past tense of "bid"	belle	a beautiful woman
bail	(1) money paid to set a person free (2) part of a wicket	berry	a fleshy fruit
		bury	to cover with earth
bale	bundle		
ball	a round object	berth	a resting place
bawl	to shout	birth	noun from verb "to be born"
baron	nobleman	blew	past tense of "blow"
barren	unproductive	blue	a colour
bare	naked	boar	wild pig
bear	(1) an animal (noun) (2) to carry, endure, put up with (verb)	bore	to make a hole (verb) to weary (verb) tidal wave (noun)
base	(1) bad (2) the bottom	bolder	more bold
bass	the lowest part in music	boulder	a rock
		brake	a retarding device
		break	to destroy
beach	the seashore	bread	baked flour
beech	a tree	bred	past tense of "breed"
bean	a plant		
been	past participle of verb "to be"	bridal	concerning a bride
beat	to strike (verb) a policeman's round (noun)	bridle	a horse's headgear (noun) to curb (verb)
beet	a root vegetable		

102

WORD	MEANING	WORD	MEANING
Britain	a country	climb	to go up
Briton	a native of Britain	clime	region or climate
by	near	coarse	rough
buy	to purchase	course	a road or track (noun)
			to pursue (verb)
canvas	strong cloth		
canvass	to ask for votes	complement	full number (noun)
			to supplement (verb)
cede	to give up	compliment	praise, flattery (noun)
seed	anything sown to produce new plants		to praise (verb)
		corps	company or unit of people
cereal	corn	corpse	dead body
serial	a story in instalments		
		council (noun)	a body for local government
check	(1) to stop (verb) (2) a ticket (noun) (3) a squared pattern (noun)	counsel	advice (noun) to advise (verb)
cheque	written promise to pay	currant	a dried fruit
		current	a stream (noun) now in use (adjective)
choir	a band of singers		
quire	24 sheets of paper		
		cymbal	a brass instrument
cite	to quote	symbol	a sign
sight	the power of seeing		
site	a place where a building stands or will stand	descent	downward motion
		dissent	to disagree
clause	part of a sentence		
claws	the nails of a beast or bird		

WORD	MEANING	WORD	MEANING
desert	to forsake (verb) a barren region (noun)	gage	something thrown down as a challenge
dessert	a sweet course	gauge	a measure
diary	a daily record of events	gilt	covered with gold
dairy	a place for the supply of milk	guilt	wrong doing
draft	(1) an order for money (2) a rough plan (3) troops	grace	mercy, charm
		graze	to feed on grass
draught	(1) air current (2) a drink	grove	a small wood
		groove	a furrow
dyeing	staining	hair	growth on the body
dying	ceasing to live	hare	a small animal
fair	(1) beautiful, just light-coloured (adj.) (2) an amusement ground (noun)	hart	a male deer
		heart	(1) the centre (2) organ of the body
fare	price of a journey		
furs	animals' coats	hoard	a hidden store
furze	gorse	horde	a gang or swarm
firs	cone-bearing trees	hole	a hollow place
		whole	entire
gait	manner of walking	human	relating to mankind
		humane	kind, compassionate
gate	an entrance	idle	doing nothing
		idol	an image
		idyll	a poem

WORD	MEANING	WORD	MEANING
incite	to urge on	manor	a lord's lands
insight	the power to see into things	manner	a way of doing something
kernel	part of a nut	mantel	a fireplace surround
colonel	chief officer of a regiment	mantle	a cloak
knight	a titled gentleman	marshal	
night	the time of darkness	(noun)	an officer
		(verb)	to arrange in order
know	to have knowledge	martial	warlike
no	negative	medal	a badge
		meddle	to interfere
lade	to load	metal	a mineral substance
laid	put in place		
latter	coming after	mettle	spirit, courage
later	following in time	mien	manner and appearance
loth	unwilling	mean	(1) to intend
loathe (verb)	to regard with disgust		(2) stingy
links	(1) rings of a chain	miner	mineworker
	(2) a golf course	minor	(1) less important
lynx	a wild cat		(2) a person under age
loose	not tight	morning	before noon
lose	{fail to keep / to be defeated}	mourning	sorrowing
magnet	device which attracts iron and points north	muscle	a part of the body
		mussel	a shell fish
magnate	wealthy or influential person	of	a pound *of* apples
		off	Get *off* the bus

WORD	MEANING	WORD	MEANING
palate	roof of the mouth	principal	most important (adj.) a chief official (noun)
palette	a painter's colour board		
pallet	a small bed	principle	a truth or rule (noun)
passed	He *passed* by	prophecy (noun)	a forecast
past	half *past* one	prophesy (verb)	to foretell
pause	to stop for a time	quiet	at rest
paws	an animal's feet	quite	entirely
pedal	a part of a machine worked by foot	reign	to rule
		rein	a strap to guide an animal
peddle	to hawk goods	rain	water from clouds
place	a particular position	road	a track
		rode	past tense of "ride"
plaice	a flat fish	rowed	past tense of "row"
plain	(1) not decorated (2) level land	rude	uncivil
plane	(1) a flat surface (2) a tool (3) a tree (4) an aircraft	rood	(1) carved screen (2) a quarter of an acre
practice	job, exercise	scene	a view
practise (verb)	I *practise* running	seen	beheld
precedent	an event that may start a new custom	sighs	deep breathing
		size	(1) extent (2) glue-like-substance
president	one who presides		

106

WORD	MEANING	WORD	MEANING
soared	past tense of "soar"	waist	part of body
		waste	to use
sword	a weapon		extravagantly
sole	(1) part of shoe	weak	not strong
	(2) a fish	week	seven days
	(3) only one		
soul	spiritual part of man, person	weather	the state of the air
		whether	which of two
stationary	standing still	wether	a male sheep
stationery	writing materials		
		whither	to which place
steal	to take another's property	wither	to fade away
steel	hardened iron	who's	who is
		whose	*Whose* house is this? i.e. to whom does it belong?
surplus	excess of		
surplice	a white gown worn by clergy and choir boys		
		wood	timber
trait	a feature	would	past tense of "will"
tray	a flat vessel with a rim		
vain	(1) conceited	yoke	neckpiece for two oxen
	(2) useless		
vane	weathercock	yolk	yellow part of an egg
vein	a blood vessel		

EXERCISES

1. Give the word which means the following:

(a) A very beautiful woman
(b) To ask for votes
(c) To give up or yield
(d) To disagree
(e) To interfere

(f) A male deer

(g) A forecast

(h) To stop for time

(i) A white gown worn by clergy and choir boys

(j) Writing materials

(k) The head of a college

(l) A person under 21 years of age

(m) A person's manner or appearance

(n) Something thrown as a challenge

(o) A kind of wild cat, very sharp-sighted

(p) A person's walk

2. From the list of words often confused write out the following sentences using the correct words in each space:

(a) He would not —— to my request.

(b) You must not —— the speed limit.

(c) The Statue of Liberty is a —— of freedom.

(d) The —— is a musical instrument.

(e) You must —— what you preach.

(f) The doctor's —— was very flourishing.

(g) The train was —— at platform number 9.

(h) The shop sold —— as well as novels.

(i) The Youth Employment Officer gave me some good ——.

(j) I —— you to ride your bicycle carefully.

(k) "You must not regard this as a ——" said my employer.

(l) Franklin D. Roosevelt was a famous —— of the United States.

3. Give a word which is spelt differently but *sounds* the same as the following:

(a) weather

(b) bridal

(c) beach

(d) berry

(e) birth

(f) cereal

(g) cheque

(h) dyeing

(i) gage

(j) kernel

(k) brake

(l) rude

(m) waist

(n) tray

(o) seen

(p) muscle

THE PHRASE AND CLAUSE

A CLAUSE is a group of words which **forms part of a sentence but contains a subject and predicate of its own.** It must therefore be distinguished from a PHRASE, which often has neither subject nor predicate. The following should make this clear:

PHRASE: *sitting on the bank*
CLAUSE: *when he was sitting on the bank*
SENTENCE: *The sun shone when he was sitting on the bank.*

There are several kinds of CLAUSES.

Some do the work of NOUNS and are called NOUN CLAUSES, e.g.:
He said *that he was going for a walk.*

Some do the work of ADJECTIVES and are called ADJECTIVAL CLAUSES, e.g.:
She returned the book *which I lent her.*

Others do the work of ADVERBS and are called ADVERBIAL CLAUSES, e.g.:
She came *when I called her.*

Let us now consider these separately.

NOUN CLAUSES usually come after a *saying* word such as *said, replied,* and *exclaimed.*
In DIRECT SPEECH the NOUN CLAUSE is put inside inverted commas.
In INDIRECT SPEECH the NOUN CLAUSE generally begins with the word *that*, e.g.:
The conductor said "*All fares, please*". (Direct Speech)
The manager said *that no credit would be allowed.* (Indirect Speech)

EXERCISES

1. State the NOUN PHRASES in the following sentences, remembering that they are always either the subject or the object of the sentence and that by itself the phrase does not make complete sense:

(a) Her complete recovery amazed us all.
(b) A posse of police arrested the criminals.
(c) My mother had heard the news of my success.
(d) Please forgive my lack of manners.
(e) The hour of his betrayal was approaching.
(f) He explained the cause of my absence.
(g) Many parents attended the annual prize-giving.
(h) Please describe the contents of the missing satchel.

2. Write out the NOUN CLAUSES in these sentences:

(a) It is certain that he will come.
(b) The master said that he was unable to accept my excuse.
(c) I exclaimed, "How ill he looks!"
(d) He hoped that I would soon recover.
(e) The boy admitted that he was guilty.
(f) He knew that he was right.
(g) The detective inquired "Tell me, how do you know this?"
(h) The teacher said "Show me what you have written."

ADJECTIVAL CLAUSES

We have seen that adjectives are words usually describing NOUNS, e.g.: a *rapid* thaw, a *slow* march, a *noisy* game.

A group of words which does the work of an adjective is called an ADJECTIVAL CLAUSE. Remember that the CLAUSE must have a SUBJECT and a PREDICATE. Adjectival clauses usually begin with the relative PRONOUNS *who, which, that, whose,* and *whom.*

Such clauses should be placed as near as possible after the noun to which they refer, e.g.:

He sent the car, which had broken down, back to the garage.

110

To say: *He sent the car back to the garage which had broken down*, is wrong, as this means the garage had broken down.
The adjectival clause commencing with *which* should follow the noun *car*.

EXERCISES

3. In these sentences replace the ADJECTIVES in italics with ADJECTIVAL CLAUSES, e.g.:

The boy extricated himself from his *ruined* bicycle.
The boy extricated himself from his bicycle *which was ruined*.

(a) The girls helped the *blind* man.
(b) The boys picked up the *fallen* branches.
(c) She wore a *silk* dress.
(d) We received some *Jaffa* oranges.
(e) He saw many *important* people.
(f) He earned a *magnificent* reward.
(g) He was a very *modest* boy.
(h) She read an *interesting* book.

ADVERBIAL CLAUSES

We have seen that a word added to a VERB or describing a verb is called an ADVERB. A group of words containing a subject and predicate used for the same purpose is called an ADVERBIAL CLAUSE.
An ADVERBIAL PHRASE does *not* contain a subject or predicate. ADVERBIAL CLAUSES are often introduced by such words as *when, where, as, before, after, although, while, unless, because, until*.

Note the following sentences:

(a) They went *before*.
(b) They went *before supper*.
(c) They went *before we had supper*.

In (a) we have an ADVERB of time *before*.
In (b) we have an ADVERBIAL PHRASE *before supper*.
In (c) we have an ADVERBIAL CLAUSE *before we had supper*.

111

EXERCISES

4. Pick out the ADVERBIAL CLAUSES in the following sentences:

(a) He arrived when I had left.
(b) He did not know where he was going.
(c) As he was ill he could not come.
(d) Although I am poor I am honest.
(e) We were happy until you came.
(f) She is older than I am.
(g) Enjoy yourselves while I am away.
(h) You will remain here until I return.
(i) I shall not go unless you give your consent.

PHRASES and CLAUSES should come close to the NOUN, VERB, or ADJECTIVE which they qualify; otherwise strange and sometimes absurd sentences may result, e.g.:

Piano for sale by gentleman with carved oak legs.

It is the *piano* which has *carved oak legs*, not the *gentleman*. Hence the sentence should be:

For sale by gentleman, piano with carved oak legs.

5. Rewrite the following sentences correctly:

(a) Wanted a boy to deliver papers with a reference.
(b) Wanted a painter who can hang paper and an apprentice.
(c) A bundle of papers has been lost by a solicitor tied up in red tape.
(d) While John was exercising his dog it bit him in the back yard.
(e) Drink freely between meals of pure water.
(f) As I was standing there she deliberately punched me on the doorstep.
(g) As Brian was going home a savage dog attacked him and bit him in the market-place.
(h) The reward my two friends were told to share between them.
(i) I saw a farmer who catches moles in Liverpool.
(j) She saw a block of flats walking down to the sea.

112

LESSON 28

COMMON EXPRESSIONS

There are many common expressions in everyday language. Here are a few of them:

The apple of one's eye
To let the cat out of the bag
A wet blanket
To cry over spilt milk
Dead beat
A chip of the old block
To put the cart before the horse
Down in the mouth
A storm in a tea-cup
At a loose end
To beat about the bush
Hard up
To pour oil on troubled waters
A feather in one's cap
A rough diamond
To play to the gallery
A red letter day
To make both ends meet
To put one's best foot forward
To live from hand to mouth
To be down at heel
To make no bones about it
To line one's pockets
To burn the candle at both ends
To go to the dogs
To have one's heart in one's mouth
To bury the hatchet
To be henpecked

To throw up the sponge
To show a clean pair of heels
To make a clean breast of something
To pay a man in his own coin
To give the cold shoulder
To throw cold water on
To turn the tables
To lead a dog's life
To let sleeping dogs lie
To have one's back to the wall
To cut someone dead
To throw dust in someone's eyes
To burn one's boats
To hit the nail on the head
To show the white feather
To face the music
On the horns of a dilemma
To be a dog in the manger
To sit on the fence
To put one's foot in it
To fall foul of
To keep one's head
To hit below the belt
To blow one's own trumpet
To kick over the traces
To blow hot and cold
To nip in the bud
To make one's mouth water

To get into hot water
To smell a rat
To play fast and loose
To shed crocodile tears
To pass the buck
To take the bull by the horns
To strike while the iron is hot
To turn up one's nose
To buy a pig in a poke
A cat on hot bricks
To eat one's words
To bury one's head in the sand
Not worth the candle
A busman's holiday
To be at the end of one's tether
To turn over a new leaf

To lead up the garden path
To keep a thing dark
A fly in the ointment
To give a dog a bad name
To keep the wolf from the door
To play the game
To tell it to the Marines
To mind one's p's and q's
To send to Coventry
To play with fire
To take forty winks
To hang one's head
To come a cropper
To kick up a dust
To have a bee in one's bonnet
To be in someone's black books
To go through the mill

EXERCISES

1. Which of the sayings has the following meaning?

(a) To act unfairly
(b) To start at the wrong end
(c) To give up
(d) To give away a secret
(e) To overdo both work and play
(f) To reverse the situation
(g) To act in a cowardly way
(h) To be in a fix or quandary
(i) To make peace
(j) To be in a desperate position
(k) To own up
(l) To make large profits for oneself
(m) To meet the worst
(n) To make a very bad mistake
(o) To be on neither side
(p) To avoid taking responsibility

114

(q) To get into trouble
(r) To make a fuss about nothing
(s) A day of importance
(t) To be absolutely right

2. (a) Which two of the list of common expressions means more or less "to ignore or scorn someone"?
(b) Give any three expressions you think might be used to express poverty.

3. Give in your own words the meaning of these expressions:
(a) The apple of one's eye
(b) A wet blanket
(c) At a loose end
(d) A chip of the old block
(e) To pay a man in his own coin
(f) To throw dust in someone's eyes
(g) To burn one's boats
(h) A dog in the manger
(i) To turn over a new leaf
(j) To lead up the garden path
(k) To keep a thing dark
(l) A fly in the ointment
(m) A cat on hot bricks

4. Here are five sayings:
   To eat humble pie
   To keep one's nose to the grindstone
   To go on a wild goose chase
   To wash one's dirty linen in public
   To turn a deaf ear

   Attach the right meaning to each of the following:
(a) To make a private quarrel known to all
(b) To go after something which isn't there
(c) To pay no attention
(d) To abase oneself
(e) To remain at work

SOME DEVICES USED IN WRITING

"How shall I write?" is just as important as "What shall I write?" A good style can only be acquired in our writing or speaking by constant practice. Food can be made more appetizing according to the way in which it is served. A room can be more pleasingly furnished by careful choice of furniture and decoration. Sound effects by B.B.C. specialists can make a play or programme more realistic and true to life.

In the same way we can make our words lively and interesting by choosing and using them well. We should try to find apt and striking ways of expressing our meaning. For instance, we often ask ourselves "What is it like?" etc., and think of some vivid comparison or likeness, such as "blind as a bat", "cunning as a fox", "light as a feather", "keen as mustard", and so on.

In such cases we are using a SIMILE. This is a **comparison between two things** and is introduced by the word LIKE or AS.

A METAPHOR is **a kind of simile with the words** *like* **or** *as* **left out**, e.g.: if we say, "He is a wolf in sheep's clothing", this is a METAPHOR. Expressed as a SIMILE this would be:

He is as treacherous as a wolf in sheep's clothing.

Any metaphor can be changed into a simile.

The English language is full of metaphors such as:

Bread is the *staff of life.*

He kept me *on tenterhooks.*

He was always *beating about the bush.*

This is a *pretty kettle of fish.*

A great many of the COMMON EXPRESSIONS used in the last chapter are metaphors.

We must, however, avoid making unsuitable comparisons, e.g.:

He put his foot down with a firm hand.

What is the use of killing the fatted calf that lays the golden eggs?

Those two sentences contain what is known as a MIXED META-PHOR, because they mix up two ideas and the result is nonsense.

EXERCISES

1. Put in the most suitable words to complete the following similes:

(a) He was as white as ——.

(b) He saw the ghost and trembled like a ——.

(c) Her hands were as cold as ——.

(d) The trunk was as heavy as ——.

(e) He was as mad as a ——.

(f) The tower stood as firm as a ——.

(g) My sister returned from her holidays as brown as a ——.

(h) The baby was as —— as —— all day.

(i) She cleaned and polished the flat. It was as —— as a ——.

(j) He came back from camping as —— as a ——.

2. Change the following METAPHORS into SIMILES:

(a) There was a *deathly silence* in the classroom.

(b) All the world's *a stage*.

(c) My young sister behaved *angelically* at school.

(d) The fog *blanketed* the town.

(e) The *torrent* of his eloquence carried away the audience.

(f) It was the *golden sunset* of the reign of Queen Victoria.

(g) The knife was *razor-sharp*.

(h) The book was *very "dry"*.

117

3. What is meant when we describe a person as:

(a) An ox?
(b) A monkey?
(c) A mouse?
(d) A lion?
(e) A fox?

(f) A rabbit?
(g) A tortoise?
(h) A mule?
(i) An oyster?
(j) A kitten?

4. What is meant by describing a person as:

(a) A Judas?
(b) A Solomon?
(c) A Shylock?
(d) A Hercules or a Samson?

(e) A Daniel?
(f) A Samaritan?
(g) A Job?
(h) An Amazon?

Sometimes a book or story is written almost entirely in the form of metaphor. Vivid comparison may be used to illustrate some special period, or moral or religious theme. This is called an ALLEGORY. Examples are: Bunyan's *Pilgrim's Progress* or Swift's *Gulliver's Travels*.

In a FABLE, a **moral is conveyed by a short story** where birds and animals are made to speak and act like human beings.

A PARABLE is a **simple story used to convey some deep religious truth** such as the "Parable of the Sower", "The Prodigal Son", etc.

The simile and metaphor are based upon comparison or likeness, but sometimes people deliberately exaggerate or express themselves in such a way as to imply an almost exactly opposite meaning.

When we illustrate by vivid contrast, we are said to be using a device known as ANTITHESIS, e.g.:
"To err is human; to forgive, divine".

IRONY is employed where words are intended to **convey an exactly opposite meaning,** as in Mark Antony's famous funeral oration over Caesar's corpse. His "ironical" words of praise for the conspirators are intended to mean exactly the reverse.

SARCASM is **a more offensive form of irony** and is intended to hurt people's feelings. It may even be disguised as a compliment, e.g.:

I know that you *always* speak the truth, is intended to mean: I know that you *never* speak the truth.

INSINUATION means **to infer or imply something,** usually unpleasant, e.g.:

You have strange ideas about honesty. (Implying, "You are actually dishonest.")

It is often difficult to distinguish it from SARCASM.

5. What device is used in the following examples?

(a) "The *evil* that men do *lives* after them,
    The *good* is oft *interred* with their bones."

(b) I really believe you are early today. (Said to a person who is usually late)

(c) "For men must *work*, and women must *weep*,
    And there's *little* to earn, and *many* to keep."

(d) Your ideas of telling the truth are well-known. (Implying that this person is very untruthful)

(e) You are always an honest boy. (Said to someone who is often dishonest)

(f) I spoke to him in sorrow rather than in anger.

Other simple FIGURES OF SPEECH are:

HYPERBOLE, that is, **deliberate exaggeration,** often used by people in everyday speech, e.g.:

I have told you *hundreds of times* not to talk during lessons.

EUPHEMISM. This is a **pleasant way of making an unpleasant statement,** e.g.:

You have told me a *fairy tale*. (i.e. a lie)

ALLITERATION. This is the **use in close succession of a number of words beginning with, or containing, the same initial letter.** It is often used in poetry, advertising and tongue-twisters, e.g.:

What we want is Watney's.
Peter Piper picked a peck of pickled peppers.

METONOMY means **a change of name,** where a thing is called not by its true name, but by something associated with it, e.g.: The pen is mightier than the sword.

ONOMATOPOEIA means using a **word which suggests the sound it represents,** e.g.:
The *whizz* of a bullet
A *ping-pong* ball

EPIGRAM. This is a **brief witty saying.** e.g.:
The only way to make dreams come true is to wake up.
I can resist everything except temptation.

(It should be distinguished from an EPITAPH which is an inscription on a gravestone, and an EPITHET which is usually one word, such as an adjective, expressing a certain quality.)

6. State briefly the name of the device or figure of speech which is used in the following:
(a) I nearly died of laughter.
(b) Mr. Brown passed away this morning.
(c) "Smith's strawberries. Sweet! Succulent! Scrumptious!"
(d) A thatcher of Thatchwood went to Thatchet a-thatching.
(e) "The double double double beat
    Of the thundering drum."
(f) Education is a continuous process from the cradle to the grave.
(g) Fire is a good servant but a bad master.

LESSON 30

SYNONYMS, ANTONYMS, HOMONYMS

A SYNONYM is a **word which has very nearly the same meaning as another word.** Many words, which seem at first sight to have the

120

same meaning, are slightly different. No two words are exactly alike; there is always some slight shade of difference in meaning, e.g., *battle, conflict, contest*. Although these words are synonyms, there is an obvious difference between them. For example, we may say:

Nelson died at the *battle* of Trafalgar.

His opinion did not *conflict* with mine.

It was a friendly *contest* of skill.

There is a well-known sentence which expresses these different shades of meaning.

One finds a *remedy* for trouble, a *cure* for disease, an *antidote* to poison.

Synonyms are useful for avoiding monotony in writing. It is often good style to use a synonym rather than repeat a word several times. The use of synonyms calls for judgement, however. Sometimes a longer, more flowery word is less effective than a simple straightforward word with the same meaning. For example, "meal" is better and less far-fetched than "collation".

Study this list and decide which of each pair of words is better for everyday speech and writing:

about	donate
approximately	give
ask	lift
enquire	elevator
beverage	pachydermatous
drink	thick-skinned
purchase	vocalist
buy	singer
commence	emporium
begin	shop

EXERCISES

1. Write down a SYNONYM for each of the following nouns:

(a) enemy
(b) interior
(c) exterior
(d) remedy
(e) raiment
(f) rank

(g) residence
(h) policeman
(i) student
(j) angler
(k) mariner
(l) terror

2. Now write a SYNONYM for each of the following adjectives:

(a) bright
(b) coarse
(c) cunning
(d) difficult
(e) enormous

(f) famous
(g) insolent
(h) feeble
(i) gruff
(j) rich

3. Select from the words on the RIGHT the word which is the best SYNONYM for the word in CAPITAL letters on the LEFT:

(a) ABANDON   (desert, abound, leave, remain, confirm)
(b) FINISHED   (planned, consented, completed, last)
(c) ELUDE   (conclude, include, escape, intrude)
(d) PERSUADE   (assuage, coax, pursue, perceive)
(e) PRAISE   (erase, honour, glorify, bless)
(f) PLEASE   (gratify, appease, satisfy, thank)
(g) JOIN   (adjourn, unite, belong, complete)
(h) PREVENT   (cure, promote, stop, preclude)

Antonyms

An ANTONYM is a word which has the **opposite meaning of another.** Unlike a synonym, it must be the **exact opposite** of a word and therefore must be the SAME PART OF SPEECH. The opposite may be a different word, such as *solid—liquid*, or it may be formed by adding a PREFIX such as *loyal—disloyal*, or by changing a SUFFIX such as *cheerful—cheerless*.

EXERCISES

4. Give the ANTONYM of each of the following:

(a) majority
(b) maximum
(c) minor
(d) wrong
(e) vanish
(f) convex
(g) negative
(h) rejoice
(i) permanent
(j) question

5. Give the ANTONYMS of the following by adding a PREFIX:

(a) moral
(b) order
(c) perfect
(d) honour
(e) sense
(f) lawful
(g) resolute
(h) truthful
(i) proper
(j) audible

6. By adding or altering the SUFFIX, give the ANTONYMS of the following:

(a) careful
(b) powerful
(c) joyful
(d) faithful
(e) tuneful
(f) merciless
(g) relent
(h) restless
(i) hopeful
(j) heedless

7. Give *different words* as ANTONYMS to the following:
   e.g.: black—white

(a) young
(b) friend
(c) rich
(d) negligent
(e) sever
(f) special
(g) lighten
(h) consider
(i) crooked
(j) condemn

Homonyms

A HOMONYM is a word that has the same *sound* as another but may have a different meaning and spelling, e.g.:

through is a homonym of *threw*
sweet is a homonym of *suite*
allowed is a homonym of *aloud*

EXERCISES

8. Write out these sentences in full, filling in the correct HOMO-NYM from the words in the brackets:
(a) The bride and bridegroom walked down the —— (isle, aisle)
(b) The climbers —— their way when the —— descended. (mist, missed)
(c) It was in —— that he tried to climb the weather ——. (vein, vain, vane)
(d) My mother could not —— up my jacket, —— I had to wear it as it was. (so, sew, sow)
(e) It was not a suitable —— for a building. (sight, cite, site)
(f) He did not care a —— what happened. (scent, cent, sent)
(g) Oh! for a —— of the crystal spring. (draft, draught)
(h) There were —— trains going —— London, but both were —— late. (to, too, two)
(i) —— you mind fetching me some ——? (wood, would)
(j) She passed —— the shop, but returned to —— some grapes. (bye, buy, by)

9. From this list insert the correct words in the sentences that follow:

their, pain, throne, cymbals, there, peace, pane, thrown, piece, symbols.

(a) The sceptre and the orb are two important State ——.
(b) Over —— are some new bricks.
(c) He was in considerable ——.
(d) "Give —— in our time O Lord."
(e) My brother plays the —— in the dance band.
(f) —— house is on fire.
(g) "This royal —— of kings, this sceptr'd isle" is a quotation from one of Shakespeare's plays

124

(h) The boy ate a small —— of cake.

(i) He broke a window ——.

(j) King William III was —— from his horse.

Many HOMONYMS are often confused. Here are some:

stationary, stationery; right, wright, rite, write; principal, principle; currant, current; practice, practise; lightning, lightening; council, counsel; weather, whether, wether.

10. Which of the words would you use in these sentences?

(a) I am going to —— on the blackboard.

(b) She was the —— boy in the pantomime.

(c) The train was —— in the railway siding.

(d) He was reading the —— issue of the magazine.

(e) The —— was very vivid.

(f) I do not know —— the —— will be fine enough for us to play cricket.

(g) I —— you to go cautiously.

(h) You must —— shooting in goal.

LESSON 31

REVISION TEST (3)

A. 1. Write down correctly the following misspelt words:

Begining	seperate	Febuary	differant
grammer	docter	alright	quarell
neccesary	recieve	allso	visiter
ocassion	cieling	Saterday	resterant
peice	goverment	usualy	libery

125

2. Rewrite these sentences correctly:

(a) A necklace of pearls, presented by friends of the bride, were among the wedding presents.

(b) The team was now in the field and about to take their place.

(c) Let you and I see to it that we do not miss the train.

(d) Who were you speaking to a minute ago?

(e) These rules do not concern you and I.

(f) Neither of them were present at morning assembly.

(g) He laid unconscious for an hour.

(h) He is the fastest swimmer of the two boys.

3. Change the following DIRECT SPEECH into REPORTED SPEECH:

(a) The teacher said, "You are wasting time, John. Come out and rewrite this work at 4 o'clock."

(b) The chairman remarked, "All this is out of order; it is beside the point, and you have taken up far too much of the committee's time."

Now change the following REPORTED SPEECH into DIRECT SPEECH.

(Remember that DIRECT SPEECH consists of words actually spoken, which must therefore be put inside inverted commas.)

(c) He asked whether the boys were ready to start.

(d) He begged them to give all the help and advice that they could.

4. What DEGREE OF COMPARISON are the following ADJECTIVES?

(a) He is a *tall* boy.

(b) He had *more* money than I had.

(c) She was wearing the *latest* design in hats.

(d) Your action was *most* creditable.

(e) It was the *lesser* of two evils.

(f) It was a *beautiful* scene.

B. 1. Rewrite the following sentences with correct punctuation, inverted commas, capital letters, etc.:

(a) the man asked have you seen the chisel yes replied his companion it is on the table

(b) a boy said to his friend are you going to the cinema no replied the other im on my way home

(c) her mother said this is the womens department shall we see if we can buy you a new hat

(d) when i return said the girl to her father will you tell me the story of the kon tiki expedition very well he replied but dont be too long at your uncles

(e) tickets please said the guard putting his head in at the window in a moment everybody was holding out a ticket they were about the same size as the people and quite seemed to fill the carriage

now then show your ticket child the guard went on looking angrily at alice and a great many voices all said together (like the chorus of a song thought alice) don't keep him waiting child why his time is worth a thousand pounds a minute

2. State the PART OF SPEECH of EACH WORD in the following sentence:

I was too old a traveller to complain but forthwith ascended by a ladder into a species of loft tolerably large and nearly empty.

3. Form as many words as you can using suitable PREFIXES with:

(a) — duct   (e) — act   (i) — late
(b) — verse   (f) — lusion   (j) — tention
(c) — approve   (g) — gress   (k) — fection
(d) — dictory   (h) — vent   (l) — trieve

C. 1. Write down words which are spelt differently but SOUND almost the same as:

(a) ate	(e) stair	(i) hail
(b) tears	(f) rye	(j) pair
(c) time	(g) waist	(k) pier
(d) aloud	(h) bare	(l) four

2. By means of a SUFFIX turn each of the following into a VERB:

(a) false	(g) solid	(m) critic
(b) hard	(h) simple	(n) emphasis
(c) soft	(i) heart	(o) familiar
(d) real	(j) length	(p) straight
(e) spark	(k) weak	
(f) liquid	(l) author	

3. What is the English equivalent to the following expressions?

(a) tête-à-tête	(f) dramatis personae
(b) entre-nous	(g) ad infinitum
(c) faux-pas	(h) nota bene
(d) locum-tenens	(i) au revoir
(e) carte blanche	(j) et cetera

4. Form ABSTRACT NOUNS from:

(a) craftsman	(i) abstain
(b) real	(j) constant
(c) false	(k) wise
(d) true	(l) just
(e) sad	(m) depart
(f) ferocious	(n) beautiful
(g) know	(o) ignorant
(h) pure	(p) intelligent

128

SIMPLE ANALYSIS AND PARSING

To analyse a sentence means "to split it up". We have seen that every sentence must have:

(a) a *subject* (the thing spoken about)
(b) a *predicate* (what is said about the subject) e.g.:

SUBJECT	PREDICATE
Fish	swim

In addition, sentences may have:

(c) AN ENLARGEMENT OF THE SUBJECT (words which tell us more about the SUBJECT)
(d) AN EXTENSION OF THE PREDICATE, e.g.:

SUBJECT		PREDICATE	
Subject	*enlargement*	*Predicate*	*extension*
Fish	of every kind	swim	in the sea

(e) AN OBJECT (that part of the sentence which answers the question "what?" after the PREDICATE), e.g.:

SUBJECT		PREDICATE		
Subject	*enlargement*	*Predicate*	*Object*	*extension*
Children	of every age	read	books	about adventure

Before analysing a sentence it is necessary to deal with the SUBJECT first, e.g.:

On the hill stood a windmill. (Here the subject *windmill* is the *last* word).

If we analyse this sentence it would be:

SUBJECT	PREDICATE	EXTENSION
A windmill	stood	on the hill

Questions should *always* be rearranged, e.g.:
What is the time?

SUBJECT	PREDICATE	EXTENSION
The time	is	what?

The SUBJECT of a COMMAND is always *you* understood, e.g.:
Bring the duster from the cupboard.

SUBJECT	PREDICATE	OBJECT	EXTENSION
You (understood)	bring	the duster	from the cupboard

Exclamations must *always* be rearranged, e.g.:
How fast time flies!

SUBJECT	PREDICATE	EXTENSION
Time	flies	(how) fast

EXERCISES

1. Analyse the following sentences:
(a) What a beautiful gown she wore!
(b) He knew nothing of it.
(c) They asked the teacher what the matter was.
(d) There is my daughter.
(e) How dirty and untidy she was!
(f) Do not make such a noise.
(g) Where are you going?
(h) Out in the stream grew many rushes.
(i) Men of every rank join the Services during war-time.
(j) The children played marbles on the way home from school.

Parsing

To parse, we consider the **exact work that every word does in a sentence** and examine its relation to other words in the sentence.
We usually do it in this way:

1. Say what part of speech the word is, (noun, verb, adjective, pronoun, etc.) remembering that words sometimes change their part of speech according to the work they do in a sentence, e.g.:
A *fast* ball. Here, *fast* is an ADJECTIVE of positive degree describing the NOUN *ball*.

130

He had a long *fast*. Here, *fast* is a COMMON NOUN, object of the verb *had*.

2. Say what *kind* of noun, verb, adjective, etc., the word is. If a noun, give its number and gender; if a verb, say whether it is transitive or intransitive and give its tense; if an adjective or adverb, give its kind and degree.

3. State *how the word is related* to some other word in the sentence.
Parse fully the sentence:

I ran to the window.
Put down the words in this sentence in a column on the left.

WORD	PART OF SPEECH	KIND	WORK DONE
I	pronoun	first person singular	subject of verb *ran*.
ran	verb	intransitive past tense, first person singular of verb *to run*.	agrees with its subject *I*.
to	preposition		governs noun *window*.
the	article	definite	qualifies noun *window*.
window	noun	common singular neuter	is governed by preposition *to*.

EXERCISES

2. Now do these simple sentences on the same plan:
(a) The smallest girl approached the two women.
(b) The cat laps milk greedily.
(c) He heard the nightingale.

131

MORE COMMON MISTAKES (1)

We have seen that many mistakes are made in the use of nouns, pronouns, and adjectives. Many more are also made with VERBS, ADVERBS, PREPOSITIONS, and CONJUNCTIONS. This, and the next, lesson will deal with some of them.

1. NON-AGREEMENT between the VERB and its SUBJECT.

(a) The boys *was* playing in the street.

A verb **must agree** with its SUBJECT in NUMBER and PERSON. The SUBJECT of the above sentence is *boys*, which is a PLURAL NOUN. Therefore the VERB must be third person plural, *were playing*. Hence we should say:

The boys *were* playing in the street.

(b) Captain Scott, as well as Admiral Byrd, *were* famous explorers.

Two NOUNS joined by *as well as, with, besides,* and *in addition to* take a SINGULAR verb when the former of the two nouns is in the singular.

Say,

Captain Scott, as well as Admiral Byrd, *was* a famous explorer.

With a COLLECTIVE NOUN either the singular or the plural may be used according to the sense we wish to convey, e.g.:

(c) All the audience stands up at once as the President enters the theatre.

After the performance the audience disperse to their various homes.

2. UNRELATED PARTICIPLES

The present participle of a verb ends in ING and often this participle is wrongly used by not referring to any particular subject, e.g.:

Knowing all the answers the exam was easy for me.

Sitting on a gate a wasp stung me.

In those two sentences the subjects, *the exam* and *a wasp*, are subjects of *was* and *stung*, but not of the participles *knowing* and *sitting*. The exam did not know the answers, nor did the wasp sit on the gate.

The sentences should be:

Since I knew all the answers, the exam was easy for me.

While I was sitting on a gate, a wasp stung me.

A sentence such as "Knowing all the answers I found the exam easy" is correct, because *I* is the subject of both *knowing* and *found*. I knew the answers, and I found the exam easy.

3. WRONG USES OF TENSES AND MOODS

(a) I done my homework in half an hour.

   Done is a past participle; the past tense *did* should be used.

(b) One day, when she was at home, she suddenly sees Helen through the window.

   The past tense *saw* should be used.

(c) I should be pleased if you *will* come.

   Should and *would* go together, so *would* must be used instead of *will* here.

(d) I shall be pleased if you *would* come.

   Shall and *will* go together, so *will* must be used instead of *would* here.

4. SPLIT INFINITIVES

The infinitive of a verb is the form with *to* in front of it, e.g.: *to skip, to enjoy, to consider*. We should try not to put other words in between. For instance do not say:

   He is going to carefully consider this. Say:

   He is going to consider this carefully.

EXERCISES

1. Rewrite these sentences correctly:

(a) The girls was all in the same netball team.

(b) Napoleon, as well as Wellington, were famous soldiers.

(c) Each boy and girl were given a bag of chocolates.

(d) Every girl must bring their thimble to the needlework class.

(e) Neither of the two boys could find their ticket.

(f) Have either of you seen my book?

(g) Each person who comes will have their own opinions.

(h) Looking round suddenly my car was passing my old friend George.

(i) The wine was not to be drank on the premises.

(j) I've been warned to continually avoid that dangerous person.

(k) I should appreciate it if you will come as early as possible.

TAUTOLOGY

This means saying the same thing twice in different words, e.g.:

(a) They came one after another in succession.

   In succession means the same as *one after another* and is unnecessary.

(b) Gradually, little by little, we forced our way through the dense forest.

   Gradually means the same as *little by little* and either the one or the other should be omitted.

(c) Although it was pouring with rain, but we went to the station to meet him.

   Do not use both *although* and *but*. One or the other should be omitted.

(d) It was pouring with rain, but, however, we went to the station to meet him.

   Do not use both *but* and *however*. One or the other should be omitted, as they both mean the same thing in that sentence.

AMBIGUITY

This means saying something which is not clear because it may have a double meaning, e.g.: John told Henry that he understood him, but he did not believe him.

It is not clear in that sentence who believed whom.

IRRELEVANCE

This means saying something which is quite unimportant to the matter being discussed; it does not apply to what we are talking about.

For example, if we are discussing the good and bad points of a certain film, and someone remarks that the ceiling of the cinema needs a new coat of paint, that remark is irrelevant to our discussion.

UNRELATED CLAUSES OR INCOMPLETE SENTENCES

Sometimes a subordinate clause is unrelated to anything spoken or written before it or after it, and this is wrong.
For example:

Because it was raining heavily when I was on my way to the airport to meet my friend. My friend's name is Enrico, which is the Italian for Henry. We first met in. . . .

The first words, *Because . . . meet my friend*, form an unrelated subordinate clause, with no other words in the same sentence to tell us what part the heavy rain had in the story. Either *because* should be omitted, which would change the subordinate clause into a complete sentence, or some more words should be added to tell us the effect of the rain on the event.

LESSON 34

MORE COMMON MISTAKES (2)

Many mistakes are made with PREPOSITIONS.

1. WRONG CASE AFTER A PREPOSITION

This sentence is incorrect:

This is strictly between you and I.

135

All prepositions must be followed by what is called the objective case of pronouns—*me, her, him, us, them.*
The correct sentence should be:

This is strictly between you and me.

Both these sentences are correct:

She likes him better than I.
She likes him better than me.

They have different meanings, however.
The first sentence means "She likes him better than I like him."
The second sentence means "She likes him better than she likes me."

2. BETWEEN can be used only when speaking of TWO people or TWO things, e.g.:

The reward was shared between Tom and Ted.

3. AMONG and AMONGST should be used when speaking of MORE THAN TWO people or things, e.g.:

The cake was shared among the four children.

4. DIFFERENT is usually followed by FROM, e.g.:

This coat is quite different from that.

But more and more people nowadays are saying *different to.* This book recommends *different from. Different than* is quite incorrect.

5. Use of AS and LIKE.

LIKE means *resembling* or *similar to* or *in the same way as,* e.g.:

A car like that must be expensive.
Your bicycle is like mine.
She looks very much like her brother.
Do it like this; if you do it like that, you will break the machine.

LIKE may be used as a noun:

I hope never to see the like of that again.

It may be used as an adjective:

You and I and other people of like feeling

It may be used as a preposition:

Do it like this.

AS must always be used after SAME, e.g.:

Mary has the same kind of watch as Dorothy.

They are the same delicious chocolate cakes as we had last week.

It is better to use AS, instead of LIKE, in front of another preposition, e.g.:

Traffic here, as in other big cities, is becoming a bigger and more confusing problem.

As on other occasions he has surprised us all again today.

Notice AS ... AS: This pen is as good as that.

CONJUNCTIONS

There are certain conjunctions that should be used together, especially EITHER—OR, NEITHER—NOR, NOT ONLY—BUT ALSO. Wrong use of EITHER—OR and NEITHER—NOR:

(a) Neither the teacher or the student was greatly interested in the lesson.

That should be:

Neither the teacher nor the student was greatly interested in the lesson.

(b) She either had the chance of telling the truth or of being dismissed.

In that sentence EITHER and OR, though used together as they should be, are incorrectly placed. They should each be put before the same part of speech.

That sentence should be:

She had the choice either of telling the truth or of being dismissed.

137

(c) He is not only anxious to acquire knowledge but also to display it.

In that sentence NOT ONLY and BUT ALSO should be put before the same part of speech:

He is anxious not only to acquire knowledge but also to display it.

(d) The reason I am telling you this is because you keep forgetting.

That sentence shows another common mistake. BECAUSE cannot be used here. You must say:

The reason I am telling you is *that* you keep forgetting.

EXERCISES

1. Rewrite the following sentences correctly:

(a) My house is different than yours.

(b) Between you and I that is a secret.

(c) The answers are in the back like in that other book.

(d) The food was shared among Brenda and Jane.

(e) Neither you or I will be asked to that party.

(f) He has the same job like his uncle had.

(g) This is very different than that.

(h) He not only wants to visit Japan, but also China.

(i) We must share this magazine among the two of us.

(j) I shall never again have as good a holiday like that.

(k) The reason for my failing the examination was because I had not worked hard enough.

(l) They came out of the playground one after another in succession.

(m) She was not only careful to wear her raincoat but also to take her umbrella.

2. Write out these sentences with the correct prepositions:

(a) I entirely disapprove —— your action.

(b) He did not wish to part —— his stamp collection.

(c) You will have to part —— your friend sooner or later.

(d) He suffered —— indigestion.

(e) I prefer the green pen —— the blue pen.

(f) They were very annoyed —— losing that match.

(g) My mother was very vexed —— me.

(h) That country is famous —— its beautiful music.

(i) He discouraged me —— any further adventures of that sort.

3. State the part of speech of each word in italics in these sentences:

(a) He left the classroom *after* I had spoken.

(b) The girl ran *after* the bus.

(c) I will go first; you follow *after*.

(d) It is a long time *since* I learnt to ride a bicycle.

(e) He entered the hall *before* I had finished speaking.

(f) Come to me *before* playtime.

(g) You should have come to me *before*.

(h) Don't cut it *like* that.

(i) John questioned Harry rudely, and Harry answered in *like* manner.

LESSON 35

ROOTS

More Suffixes and Prefixes

A ROOT of a word is **the main part or stem** to which we add the PREFIX, SUFFIX or both. Many of the word roots in our language are derived from LATIN and FRENCH, e.g.: from the Latin root *audio*, meaning "I hear", many English words are formed, such as: audible, audience, audit, audition, auditor.

EXERCISE

1. Form as many English words as you can of any kind from these LATIN ROOTS (NOUNS):

WORD	MEANING
aqua	water
manus	hand
navis	ship
herba	grass
pecunia	money
veritas	truth

2. Now do the same with these LATIN ROOTS (ADJECTIVES):

WORD	MEANING
fortis	strong
liber	free
plus	more
primus	first
flexibilis	flexible
frigidus	cool
quadratus	square

3. Here are some LATIN verbs. They are the ROOTS of many English words, such as PORTO = "I carry", which gives at least ten English words, such as: import, export, deport, support, report, porter, portable, transport, important, portfolio, portmanteau.

   Form as many English words as you can from the following LATIN verbs:

WORD	MEANING
abduco	I carry off
absolvo	I set free
capio	I take
clamo	I shout
curro	I run

dico	I say
facio	I make
mitto	I send
pendeo	I hang
rego	I rule
scribo	I write
teneo	I hold
venio	I come
voco	I call

4. The meaning of many English words can also be found in certain FRENCH verbs, e.g.: the French word PENSER = "to think" gives us the English word "pensive" meaning "thoughtful".

Give English words which are very similar to each of these FRENCH verbs:

WORD	MEANING
promener	to walk
chanter	to sing
fumer	to smoke
habiter	to dwell
sentir	to feel
donner	to give
élever	to rise
parler	to speak
monter	to climb

SUFFIXES, especially -er and -est, are often used when we make new words to form the comparative and superlative adjectives, e.g.:

long, longer, longest.

Suffixes are also used when we make adjectives from nouns, e.g.: gold, golden; truth, truthful; east, eastern; Hercules, Herculean; friend, friendly; boy, boyish; joy, joyous; trouble, troublesome.

141

5. From the preceding list place the most suitable word in these sentences:

(a) A wedding is usually a very —— occasion.
(b) —— relations were broken off between the two countries.
(c) This is a feat of —— strength.
(d) It was a —— sunset.
(e) He had a very —— cough.
(f) The boy made a —— statement.
(g) The —— counties of England are drier than those of the west.
(h) It was a very —— prank to play.

SUFFIXES meaning "little" or "small" can also be used to make what are known as DIMINUTIVES. Here are thirteen such diminutives, formed from eight suffixes:

SUFFIX	DIMINUTIVE
—ing	duckling
—kin	manikin, pannikin
—ock	hillock, bullock
—ule	globule, granule
—let	droplet, piglet, twiglet
—et	casket
—ette	rosette
—en	kitten

6. Form DIMINUTIVES by adding a SUFFIX to these words:

(a) cigar
(b) brook
(c) lamb
(d) maid
(e) book
(f) wave
(g) stream
(h) river

142

7. To the following adjectives add SUFFIXES to turn them into ABSTRACT NOUNS. Remember that an abstract noun is the name of a quality or state, e.g.: adjective: *wicked*; abstract noun: *wickedness*.

(a) sad
(b) helpful
(c) simple
(d) difficult

(e) cruel
(f) mad
(g) rash
(h) wise

8. Now add SUFFIXES to the following adjectives to form VERBS:

(a) weak
(b) civil
(c) vital
(d) sharp
(e) soft

(f) brutal
(g) quick
(h) strong
(i) visual
(j) despicable

9. Here is a list of SUFFIXES concerned with occupations:

—er, —or, —ist, —ian, —ar, —eer, —wright, —ary, —ant, —ier.

Using these suffixes, write down the occupation of the person who does the following:

(a) is employed to write letters
(b) mends burst pipes
(c) sells articles at the door
(d) paints pictures
(e) commands a brigade
(f) is skilled in the building of ships
(g) rents a house
(h) sells articles to the highest bidder
(i) is skilled in music
(j) attends sick people
(k) cares for teeth
(l) sells furs

143

LESSON 36

THE USE OF THE DICTIONARY

In any English exercise we should always have a dictionary at hand for reference. This enables us to find out not only the spelling of a word, but also its correct part of speech, its meaning, derivation, and pronunciation.

It is important to remember that all words in a dictionary are arranged in alphabetical order. This means arranging words according to the order of their initial letters, then their second letters, their third letters, and so on.

Thus, (a) *avoid, brilliant, companion, delicious, evening* are arranged according to the initial letters only—a, b, c, d, e.

(b) *avoid, awning, axle, aye, azure* are arranged in the order of their second letters—v, w, x, y, z—since the initial letter A is the same for all those words.

(c) *plateau, platen, platform, plating, platinum, platoon* are arranged (i) in the order of the fifth letters since the first four letters PLAT are the same for all; (ii) in the order of the sixth letters with *plateau* and *platen*, and also with *plating* and *platinum*.

(d) *cloud, drip, droop, drop, fellow, follow, ill* are arranged, first, in order of initial letters; then *drip, droop, drop* are arranged in order of first and second letters, then in order of third letters; and so on.

EXERCISES

1. Arrange these words in full alphabetical order:

   prolong, often, oil, power, powerful, curate, cure, hold, buzz, buy, aid, air, volley, toil, space, pipe, pitch, pit, hole, powder.

2. Arrange these words in full alphabetical order:

   he, hazard, hawser, haze, hay, hazy, hawthorn, hazel, hazardous, head, hayward.

A good dictionary gives not only the alphabetical order of words
—which is also the spelling of each word—but also each word's

(i) pronunciation
(ii) part of speech
(iii) meaning
(iv) derivation.

Thus:

SUPERB (syooperb or sooperb): a. impressive, splendid, grand
(L. *superbus*, proud).

The first words in brackets show that the SU is to be pronounced
as in *soon*, not as in *sun*.
The "a" denotes "adjective".
The L denotes "Latin".

CATASTROPHE (cata'strof*ee*): n. disastrous end, ruin. (Gk. *cata*,
down; *strophe*, turn).

The mark after the second "a" in the bracketed pronunciation
shows that the word is stressed or accented on the second syllable—the syllable immediately before the mark; the "ta" is
spoken more strongly than the other parts of the word.
The "n" denotes "noun". Gk. denotes Greek.

All dictionaries do not show or explain pronunciation in the
same way. Some dictionaries use what are called "phonetic"
signs to show pronunciation, and the person using the dictionary
has to refer to a list of these signs at the beginning of the book.

Have a good look at your own dictionary, and try to understand how it shows pronunciation, meanings, parts of speech,
and derivations.

EXERCISES

3. Use a dictionary to separate these words into two groups, the
one where ANTI means "against" and the other derived from
ANTE which means "before".
(a) antidote
(b) anticipate

(c) antique
(d) antipathy
(e) anticyclone
(f) antiquarian
(g) antiseptic

4. Look up in your dictionary the word AUTO used as a prefix and derived from a Greek word meaning "self", and find words beginning with AUTO to describe the following:

(a) The story of one's own life.
(b) An absolute ruler.
(c) A person's own signature.
(d) The right of self-government.
(e) Something self-acting or self-working.

5. With the help of your dictionary, answer these questions, and explain the meaning of each word in italics:

(a) Is water *inflammable*?
(b) Which of these is probably *colossal:* speck, skyscraper, scrap, serenade?
(c) Is sunshine *edible*?
(d) Does an *isotherm* connect places of the same height, wind, pressure, or temperature?
(e) Is your writing *audible* or *legible*?
(f) Is a *telephone* a musical instrument? What word ending in PHONE is a musical instrument?
(g) Where would you expect to find an *epitaph*?
(h) Is an *escarpment* when a person escapes from prison?
(i) Is *encumber* a kind of cucumber?
(j) Would you say that Christmas is a festival which is *annual* or *perennial*?

6. Where to find things out:

Album, atlas, biography, calendar, catalogue, diary, dictionary, directory, newspaper, timetable.

Which of those would you look in to find out the following?

(a) The address of a person
(b) The time of a train or bus
(c) A list of goods priced
(d) An account of the events of the previous day
(e) The date and day of the month
(f) The position of a port
(g) A collection of photographs or autographs
(h) The life story of some one as told by another person
(i) The meaning of "onomatopoeia"
(j) The day on which a boy or girl first learnt to ride a bicycle

LESSON 37

IDIOMS, COLLOQUIALISMS, CLICHÉS AND SLANG

Idioms

Every language has a great many **special words and phrases which have some particular significance and are known as "idioms"**. English is full of idioms and idiomatic expressions, which are very difficult for the foreigner to grasp, as often he has no similar phrase in his own language to express this idiomatic use of words.

Many idioms which we still use today were first created by Shakespeare or by the early translators of the Bible into English, e.g., "the arm of the law", "I haven't slept a wink", "I escaped by the skin of my teeth".

In using idiomatic phrases we must make sure that the currently-accepted meaning is clearly understood; for example, to *make shift* with something is not quite the same as a *makeshift arrangement*. *To overlook something* is not the same as *to look over* it.

147

Idioms often evade or ignore the accepted rules of grammar. Most of them are metaphors and many of the "common expressions" used in a previous lesson are in fact idioms.

Here are a few examples of idiomatic expressions:

To bear in mind (to remember)
To put up with (to tolerate)
To make out (to understand)
To take over (to take charge)
To come round (to recover consciousness)
To go into a matter (to examine or investigate)

EXERCISES

A great many English words can be used idiomatically, for example, the verb TO BEAR. We say "*to bear* a charmed life" which means "to be fortunate in escaping disaster".

1. The following phrases all contain the verb TO BEAR. Give the idiomatic expressions used for:
(a) To tell lies about a person
(b) To retain angry feelings
(c) To keep in one's memory
(d) To confirm or support
(e) To keep up one's spirits
(f) To endure
(g) To take the blame or biggest strain
(h) To harbour resentment against someone

2. Give the meaning of the following idiomatic expressions which all contain the word BACK:
(a) To back out of
(b) To break the back of
(c) To back up
(d) To go back on one's word
(e) To hang back
(f) To put one's back up

(g) When one's back is turned
(h) To put one's back into something

3. The following idiomatic phrases all contain the word FACE. For example: If I *face up* to my difficulties, I meet them with courage and determination.

Give the phrases or expressions containing the word FACE which mean:

(a) To endure to the end
(b) The nominal value of an object
(c) Have the audacity or effrontery
(d) Not to laugh
(e) As a thing appears
(f) To look rather miserable
(g) To be apparently courageous
(h) To be strongly opposed
(i) Not to shrink from what is coming

Colloquialisms

These are closely allied to idioms and often difficult to distinguish. A colloquialism is an **expression or group of words used in popular or familiar speech with a very different meaning from that which it would bear in more formal language.** Thus a person who is said "to be crazy" about something is not mad or insane, but is *very fond* of it. We may say that a person who attempts something "has a shot at it".

4. Give the popular expressions which are the equivalent of the following:

(a) To be in trouble
(b) Deeply involved
(c) To make the utmost effort
(d) To be exhausted
(e) To be in poor health
(f) It is your responsibility

Clichés

A cliché is **an expression which was striking or specially amusing or interesting when it was first spoken or written, but which has become so over-used since then that it is no longer amusing or interesting;** in fact it has become boring or even irritating from too much constant repetition.

Clichés, like colloquialisms and slang, vary from period to period of history. "The cup that cheers" was once an overworked cliché for "a cup of tea". In recent years "the sixty-four thousand dollar question" has become an irritating cliché for "the most important question".

A cliché is different from a colloquialism or slang. The former means what it says; "the sixty four thousand dollar question" clearly means a valuable or important question. The latter usually means something different from the normal meaning of the word or words; "smashing", when used as a popular modern word of slang, means "wonderful", not "destructive", which is the normal meaning of the verb "to smash".

Slang and Jargon

A slang expression is very much like a colloquialism. Probably the only difference between a slang expression and a colloquial expression is that the latter is older and more widely understood and used. "Crazy", with the meaning of "enthusiastic", is more colloquial than slang since it has been used with that meaning for much longer than "nuts", with the meaning of "enthusiastic", and is more widely used than "nuts". "He is crazy about music" is understood by more people, and especially by old people, than "He is nuts on music."

Most slang expressions die sooner rather than later. Some only last for a single year. Some last many years and become no longer really slang, but idioms as firmly established and understood as "to back a horse" (first used by Shakespeare, so far as is known), "to put up with", "to keep a straight face", and "bus" which is now standard English.

150

Slang is all right between friends, particularly friends of equal age or equal standing. It is all right in a very friendly letter to someone of one's own age or position. It should be avoided, however, in formal speech and in a formal letter and when it is little likely to be appreciated or understood.

Different regions of the same country, different age-groups of people, different workers in the same trade, may have different slang expressions. Many professional expressions become what is called "jargon". Someone who speaks or writes only in his own particular professional jargon is as irritating as the person who fills his talk with clichés, for example, the economist who speaks of the "lower age-groups in the middle-income brackets", meaning "young people who earn average wages", in his everyday conversations with friends who may not be economists.

Other examples of jargon occur in newspapers, radio and television where certain words and phrases become fashionable and over-worked, e.g.: "escalate", "environmental", "major breakthrough", "at this point in time".

EXERCISES

5. Can you pick out the idioms, the slang, and the jargon here?

(a) controlled zero population growth
(b) Stop messing around. Buzz off.
(c) I'll bear it in mind.
(d) He took to his heels.

LESSON 38

PROVERBS

There are thousands of proverbs or wise sayings in the English language. You have probably heard many of the following:

1. Actions speak louder than words.
2. A bird in the hand is worth two in the bush.

3. Absence makes the heart grow fonder.
4. A cat may look at a king.
5. A creaking gate hangs longest on its hinges.
6. A drowning man clutches at a straw.
7. A friend in need is a friend indeed.
8. All's well that ends well.
9. As well be hanged for a sheep as a lamb.
10. An apple a day keeps the doctor away.
11. A miss is as good as a mile.
12. A rolling stone gathers no moss.
13. A stitch in time saves nine.
14. A good conscience is a continual feast.
15. A good example is the best sermon.
16. A fool and his money are soon parted.
17. An Englishman's home is his castle.
18. All that glitters is not gold.
19. An honest look covereth many faults.
20. An ounce of common sense is worth a king's ransom.
21. A thing too much seen is little prized.
22. A living dog is better than a dead lion.
23. A little learning is a dangerous thing.
24. A liar is not believed when he speaks the truth.
25. A light purse makes a heavy heart.
26. As you make your bed so must you lie on it.
27. A man is as old as he feels and a woman as old as she looks.
28. Birds of a feather flock together.
29. Beauty is only skin deep.
30. Blood is thicker than water.
31. Brevity is the soul of wit.
32. Charity covers a multitude of sins.
33. Charity begins at home.
34. Cut your coat according to your cloth.
35. Discretion is the better part of valour.
36. Don't count your chickens before they are hatched.
37. Don't halloo until you are out of the wood.
38. Empty vessels make most noise.
39. Every dog has his day.

40. Evil communications corrupt good manners.
41. Enough is as good as a feast.
42. Every cloud has a silver lining.
43. Evil weeds grow apace.
44. Every man is the architect of his own fortune.
45. Example is better than precept.
46. Exchange is no robbery.
47. Familiarity breeds contempt.
48. Fine feathers make fine birds.
49. Forewarned is forearmed.
50. Fools rush in where angels fear to tread.
51. Fine words butter no parsnips.
52. First come first served.
53. Fire is a good servant but a bad master.
54. Great minds think alike.
55. Good wine needs no bush.
56. Great oaks from little acorns grow.
57. Good and quickly seldom meet.
58. Handsome is that handsome does.
59. Hard words break no bones.
60. Honesty is the best policy.
61. Hunger finds no fault with the cooking.
62. Half a loaf is better than no bread.
63. He laughs best who laughs last.
64. He who laughs last laughs longest.
65. He pays the piper who calls the tune.
66. Imitation is the sincerest form of flattery.
67. It's an ill wind that blows nobody any good.
68. It's a long lane that has no turning.
69. In for a penny in for a pound.
70. Little pitchers have great ears.
71. Listeners hear no good of themselves.
72. Laugh and the world laughs with you; weep and you weep alone.
73. Least said soonest mended.
74. Look before you leap.
75. Let sleeping dogs lie.

76. Leave well alone.
77. Laugh and grow fat.
78. Let not the pot call the kettle black.
79. Manners maketh man.
80. Marry in haste and repent at leisure.
81. Make hay while the sun shines.
82. More haste less speed.
83. Necessity is the mother of invention.
84. Necessity knows no law.
85. Needs must when the devil drives.
86. No man can serve two masters.
87. Nothing succeeds like success.
88. Nothing venture nothing win.
89. No news is good news.
90. New brooms sweep clean.
91. One good turn deserves another.
92. One man's meat is another man's poison.
93. Possession is nine-tenths of the law.
94. Penny wise pound foolish.
95. Prevention is better than cure.
96. The early bird catches the worm.
97. Too many cooks spoil the broth.
98. Self-praise is no recommendation.
99. Still waters run deep.
100. Where there's a will there's a way.

EXERCISES

1. What proverbs mean more or less the same as the following?
(a) The early bird catches the worm.
(b) Let sleeping dogs lie.
(c) More haste less speed.
(d) To the hungry no bread is bad.
(e) A good example is the best sermon.

2. Certain proverbs contain what might be termed "opposites":

e.g., *Laugh* and the world laughs with you; *weep* and you weep alone.

Write out any eight such proverbs.

3. Which proverb would you quote:

(a) To a person extravagant beyond his means?

(b) To a weary traveller?

(c) To an ailing person who thinks he won't live to a good old age?

(d) To a very "long-winded" person who takes a considerable time to tell a joke or relate a funny story?

(e) To a person who goes from one job to another?

(f) To a person who resorts to flattery?

(g) To a noisy class of children?

(h) To a person in need of encouragement?

(i) To a boaster?

4. Which proverbs do you think mean the following?

(a) Appearances are not all they seem to be.

(b) People of the same tastes and inclinations often associate together.

(c) You must put up with the consequences of your own actions.

(d) By taking precautions in time you can often save further trouble.

(e) There is hope even in the worst circumstances.

(f) Make the fullest use of your opportunities while you have the chance.

(g) Consider well before you take a decisive step.

(h) A person in a new job may make drastic changes.

(i) If too many people try to do the same job at the same time, they may spoil the result.

(j) A good product needs no advertisement.

5. Write down any six proverbs which refer to birds or animals.

WHAT WE HAVE LEARNT

Vocabulary

Vocabulary is simply a person's stock of words.
One's vocabulary may be increased by:

(a) Reading intelligently.
(b) The constant use of a dictionary.
(c) Listening to others.

Sentences and Phrases

A sentence is a complete thought expressed in words. It generally begins with a capital letter and must end with a full stop. Every sentence should contain a SUBJECT or name, and a PREDICATE or what is said about the SUBJECT.

The chief kinds of sentence are:

(a) SIMPLE STATEMENTS
(b) QUESTIONS
(c) COMMANDS
(d) REQUESTS AND DESIRES
(e) THOSE EXPRESSING SURPRISE OR EXCLAMATION

A PHRASE is a group of words which does not make a complete statement, as it does not contain a finite verb.
A CLAUSE is a group of words which forms part of a sentence and generally has a subject and predicate of its own.

Parts of Speech

There are EIGHT parts of speech consisting of:

NOUNS	VERBS	PREPOSITIONS
PRONOUNS	ADVERBS	CONJUNCTIONS
ADJECTIVES	INTERJECTIONS	

156

Note: INTERJECTIONS are merely exclamations and do not always count as parts of speech.

Nouns are divided into:

PROPER NOUNS. (Names of *special* people, places, or things, and must always be written with CAPITAL LETTERS at the beginning.)

COMMON NOUNS are the names which objects have "in common" with all other objects of the same class. The word COMMON really means "shared by all".

COLLECTIVE NOUNS refer to a number of persons, things, or animals regarded as a single group of the same kind, e.g.: flock, crowd, etc.

ABSTRACT NOUNS are the names of special qualities, conditions, or emotions. They really name things we cannot see, touch, or smell, e.g.: beauty, cruelty, pity, etc.

When a noun refers to ONE object it is said to be SINGULAR.
When it refers to MORE THAN ONE object, it is said to be PLURAL.

NOUNS have four GENDERS:

MASCULINE	(male)
FEMININE	(female)
NEUTER	(neither)
COMMON	(referring to both sexes)

Pronouns

A pronoun is a word that stands FOR a noun.
The main kinds are:

(a) PERSONAL standing for the three persons:

The first person or person speaking (*I, me, we, us*)
The second person, the person or things spoken to (*Thou, thee, you, ye*)
The third person, the person or thing spoken about (*He, him, her, she, it, they, them*)

157

(b) POSSESSIVE simply show possession:

> The first person (*Mine, ours, etc.*)
> The second person (*Thine, yours,* etc.)
> The third person (*His, hers, theirs, etc.*)

(c) RELATIVE such as: *who, whom, whose*, etc.

(d) INTERROGATIVE ask questions, *who? which? what?* etc.
Who is it? Whose is it?

(e) DEMONSTRATIVE point out things, e.g., *this* and *that*.
Likewise they are *not* accompanied by a noun, e.g., *This* is
for sale but *that* is not.

(f) INDEFINITE PRONOUNS refer to things in a vague and general
way, e.g.: *any, anything, anybody*, etc.
Again, we must *not* use these words to describe nouns.
You use an indefinite pronoun in a sentence like this:
Anything can happen.

Adjectives

An adjective describes or limits a noun or pronoun.
Chief classes:

(a) DEMONSTRATIVE used before a noun and point out. They
answer the question "Which?", e.g., *That* chair. *This* picture, etc.

(b) POSSESSIVE: e.g., *My* friend, *Your* face. *Our* garden, etc.

(c) QUALITY: These tell what sort or kind, e.g., A *heavy* coat. A
keen wind, etc.

(d) QUANTITY or NUMBER: Tell how many or how much, e.g.:

> (1) There were *three* cups.
> (2) He drank *some* water.

(e) INTERROGATIVE: These ask a question and again must be
accompanied by a noun, e.g.:

> (1) *Which* way did he go?
> (2) *What* answer did he give?

The Articles

These are really demonstrative adjectives as they point out a NOUN. A and AN are the INDEFINITE articles as they point out no special thing.

THE is the DEFINITE article referring to a special person or thing. Generally AN is used before nouns which begin with one of the vowels: a, e, i, o, u, e.g., AN apple, AN egg, etc.

A is used before nouns beginning with a consonant, e.g., A box, A cup, etc.

ADJECTIVES have THREE DEGREES OF COMPARISON:

POSITIVE	COMPARATIVE	SUPERLATIVE
tall	taller	tallest
	OR more tall	OR most tall

Note: One or other of these forms must be used but not both. We must *not* say, "*more* taller" or "*most* tallest".

Verbs

A verb is a *doing, saying,* or *thinking* word.

A verb is TRANSITIVE when it needs an OBJECT to make complete sense, e.g.: He broke a *window* (object).

An INTRANSITIVE verb makes a complete statement and does NOT require an OBJECT.

(1) The bird sings.
(2) The fire burns.

Transitive verbs may be:

(1) ACTIVE when the SUBJECT performs the action, e.g.:
    The cat laps milk.

(2) PASSIVE when the SUBJECT has the action done to it, e.g.:
    Milk is lapped by the cat.

The two chief AUXILIARY or helping verbs are:
TO BE and TO HAVE.

The MOOD of a verb denotes the way in which a statement is made.

(a) The INDICATIVE MOOD simply makes a statement, or asks a question, e.g.:

   I always *look* both ways before I *cross* the road.

(b) The IMPERATIVE MOOD expresses a command or request, e.g.: *Stop! Look! Think!* before you cross the road.

(c) The SUBJUNCTIVE MOOD expresses a condition, wish, or doubt, e.g.:

   If I *were* you I *should wear* an overcoat.

Tense   The tense of a verb means the TIME which it expresses. The three main TENSES of all verbs are:

PRESENT   e.g.: It rains, *or* It is raining.
PAST   e.g.: It rained, *or* It was raining.
FUTURE   e.g.: It will rain.

VERBS have NUMBER. They are either SINGULAR or PLURAL and must agree with their SUBJECT.

Special Parts of the Verb

(a) The INFINITIVE has the word *to* in front of it, e.g.: *to run.*

(b) PRESENT PARTICIPLE: running.

(c) PAST PARTICIPLE: run.

   (In the INFINITIVE the *to* must not be separated from the other part of the verb, otherwise we have a SPLIT INFINITIVE, e.g., to swiftly run, which is not considered good English. Say: to run swiftly.)

   The present participle must be RELATED to a NOUN or PRONOUN.

Adverbs

An adverb is a word which modifies or limits a verb, adjective, another adverb, a preposition or a conjunction.

Adverbs may be classified as follows:

(a) Adverbs of MANNER answering the question "how?" e.g.:
   He ran *swiftly*.
(b) Adverbs of TIME answering the question "when?" e.g.:
   He will be going *soon*.
(c) Adverbs of PLACE answering the question "where?" e.g.:
   He is not *here*.
(d) Adverbs of DEGREE answering the question "to what extent?" e.g.:
   I was *nearly* exhausted.

Prepositions

A preposition is a word used before a noun or pronoun to show its relation to some other word in the sentence which it is said to govern, e.g.:

He remained *behind* the door.

Conjunctions

A conjunction is a word that joins together other words or groups of words.

Conjunctions most frequently used are *and, but,* and *so, either——or, neither——nor, not only——but also.*

Interjections are exclamations such as Oh! Ha! Alas!

DIRECT SPEECH consists of the actual words used by a speaker and must be put inside inverted commas, e.g.:

"I usually get up at 7.30 a.m."

INDIRECT or REPORTED SPEECH gives the remarks of the speaker as quoted by someone else and is introduced by a verb of saying in the PAST TENSE, e.g.:

He said that he usually got up at 7.30 a.m.

161

A PREFIX is a single letter or syllable added to the BEGINNING of a word, e.g.:

dis-content.

A SUFFIX is a letter or syllable added to the END of a word, e.g.:

exist-ence.

Some Simple "Figures of Speech"

A SIMILE is a likeness or comparison introduced by the words like, or as, e.g.:

"blind as a bat"
"like a ball of fire"

A METAPHOR is an implied simile not introduced by like or as, e.g.:

Bread is the staff of life.

ANTITHESIS is illustration by vivid contrast, e.g.:

I speak to thee in sorrow, not in anger.

HYPERBOLE is deliberate exaggeration, e.g.:

I have told you hundreds of times.

EUPHEMISM is a pleasant way of making an unpleasant statement, e.g.:

Mrs. Davison's cat was put to sleep (killed without pain).

METONOMY is a change of name when a thing is called not by its true name but by something closely associated with it, e.g.:

The House of Commons was in an uproar. (i.e. the members of the House were in an uproar).

ONOMATOPOEIA is the use of a word which suggests the sound it represents, e.g.:

The crack of a whip. The buzzing of bees, etc.

162

LESSON 40

GENERAL REVISION TEST

A. 1. There was a heavy rainstorm in Birmingham last night.

(a) State whether this sentence is a command, statement or question.

(b) Name the PROPER NOUN.

(c) Name the COMMON NOUNS.

(d) State whether *heavy* is an ADJECTIVE or ADVERB.

(e) What is the VERB in this sentence? Give its TENSE.

(f) Name the PREPOSITION.

(g) What part of speech is *last*?

2. The following sentences contain a NOUN, ADJECTIVAL or an ADVERBIAL CLAUSE. Write out the clause in each sentence and state its kind:

(a) We will remain until you arrive.

(b) The teacher said that the whole class would have to stay in.

(c) I have found the pen which I had lost.

(d) As I was returning home I saw the detective.

(e) Tell me what you have done.

(f) We have a dog that can sit up and beg.

(g) I remarked how ill she looked.

(h) I am going to give a prize to the boy or girl whose essay is the best.

(i) She arrived after I had gone.

(j) He told me that I stood a good chance of passing the examination.

3. What are the common expressions that can be used to describe the following?

(a) To act without delay

(b) To give away a secret

(c) To do something in the wrong order
(d) To be continually "nagged" by one's wife
(e) To lead a very wretched life
(f) To make peace
(g) To get away quickly
(h) To mislead somebody

4. Give ONE WORD for the following:

(a) Deliberately to set fire to a building
(b) To tell a lie in a law court
(c) To die by suffocation
(d) An assumed name
(e) The murder of a brother or sister
(f) A fertile spot in a desert
(g) A planet or similar body revolving round another
(h) Transmitting sound and pictures through the air

B. 1. There is a word which SOUNDS the same but is SPELT differently from the following. Name the word and state what part of speech it is.

(a) haul
(b) practise
(c) ascent
(d) bury
(e) mourning
(f) principle
(g) tray
(h) whether
(i) sword
(j) scene

2. In the following words a certain letter is "silent". What is the letter?

(a) victuals
(b) gnash
(c) honest
(d) knuckle
(e) yolk
(f) autumn
(g) glisten
(h) write
(i) calm
(j) hymn
(k) honour
(l) wreath

3. The following words end in —ORY, —ARY, or —ERY. Write them out in full.

(a) mission—
(b) laborat—
(c) gran—
(d) brav—
(e) tempor—
(f) fact—
(g) necess—
(h) mem—
(i) cel—
(j) not—
(k) lavat—
(l) groc—
(m) promont—
(n) artill—
(o) advers—
(p) contr—
(q) vict—
(r) surg—

4. Give the meaning of the PREFIXES in the following words and state from which language they are derived:

(a) amphibious
(b) retrograde
(c) perimeter
(d) polygon
(e) contravene
(f) automatic
(g) antibiotic
(h) television
(i) equidistant
(j) bemoan

5. What do we call a person:

(a) Who is devoted especially to the delights of food and drink?
(b) Who has the reputation of bringing bad luck?
(c) Who always looks on the black side of things?
(d) Who is a very narrow-minded person?
(e) Who is a very strict disciplinarian?
(f) Who is very inscrutable or mysterious?
(g) Who engages in rather foolish or romantic adventures?
(h) Who shows extreme courage and endurance?

C. 1. Which of these pairs of words is the right one to use in each of the following sentences?

(a) He found the (quay, key) of the door down by the (key, quay) side.
(b) This (sealing, ceiling) wax is the same colour as the (sealing, ceiling) of the room.
(c) He will (break, brake) his ankle if he is not careful when stepping out of the shooting (break, brake).
(d) He (through, threw) the ball (threw, through) the window.

(e) I am very fond of a (peace, piece) of tender (stake, steak).
(f) We (where were) going home last night when we saw a (you, yew, ewe) under a (you, yew, ewe) tree.

2. Give ONE WORD for a person:
(a) Who collects stamps
(b) Who stuffs animals
(c) Who uses both hands equally well
(d) Who compiles maps
(e) Who brings a law-suit into court against someone else
(f) Who is equally at home in any country
(g) Who listens uninvited to private conversations
(h) Who is recovering from an illness
(i) Who pretends to be what he is not
(j) Who deals with mental illness or disorders

3. The following words, whose meanings are given, end in —ANCE or —ENCE.
   Give the appropriate word for:
(a) The use of too much of anything.
(b) Quickness of understanding.
(c) Watchfulness.
(d) The act of being sorry for one's sins.
(e) A person's moral sense of right and wrong.
(f) Help rendered.
(g) A complete thought expressed in words.
(h) A building in which a person lives.
(i) A state of wealth.
(j) Bearing with somebody or something.

4. What LITERARY DEVICES are used in these sentences?
(a) A word fitly spoken is like apples of gold in pictures of silver.
(b) "Say not a word, for the pen of happiness hath written on thy face the ode of gratitude."
(c) The words of a tale-bearer are as wounds.
(d) The day I first learnt to ride a bicycle was a red-letter day in my life.

166

(e) Speech is silver; silence is golden.

(f) "There are millions of examples of this rule," she said.

(g) "How sleep the brave:
    The brave that are no more."

(h) "Here under leave of Brutus and the rest—
    For Brutus is an honourable man:
    So are they all, all honourable men—
    Come I to speak in Caesar's funeral." (Mark Antony)

(i) She nearly died of laughter.

(j) I think you have made a slight mistake (said to a person who has made a big mistake).

5. Which are the nouns, and which are the verbs, here?

(a) advice
(b) choice
(c) devise
(d) practice
(e) practise
(f) device
(g) advise
(h) choose

6. What is at fault in each of these passages?

(a) With powerful wings he flew like a lion to the rescue of his friend.

(b) This firmly solid United Nations building, as it moves along the road of progress, will sweep away the evil winds of international hatred.

(c) Just as we water each branch of a tree separately in order that the whole tree may grow well, so we must provide money for each separate department of this school in order that the whole school may develop well.

7. What adjectives do we use for:

(a) a person who cannot see?

(b) a thing which cannot be seen?

(c) a person who cannot hear?

(d) a thing which cannot be heard?

(e) a person who has not learnt to write?

(f) writing which is impossible to read?

167

(g) a person who readily believes anything?

(h) a thing which is difficult or impossible to believe?

8. What did this confused clergyman really mean to say?

Dear people, as the room upstairs is champ and dilly, the meeting will be halled in the hell below.

9. Write this, adding all necessary punctuation, apostrophes, and capital letters:

though im ill ill write to miss green i miss miss green before she went to new york she helped me a lot with my mathematics i still have miss greens green pen she gave it to me when she left me ill use it to write to her now

10. Add adjectives and abstract nouns, e.g.:

optimist
optimistic (adjective)
optimism (abstract noun: showing the attitude of an optimist)

(a) politician
.... (adjective)
.... (the interest of a politician)

(b) villain
.... (adjective)
.... (the act of a villain)

(c) hero
.... (adjective)
.... (the behaviour of a hero)

(d) friend
.... (adjective)
.... (being a friend)

(e) coward
.... (adjective)
.... (the act of a coward)

(f) child
.... (adjective)
.... (the time when one is a child)